Waterfront Development

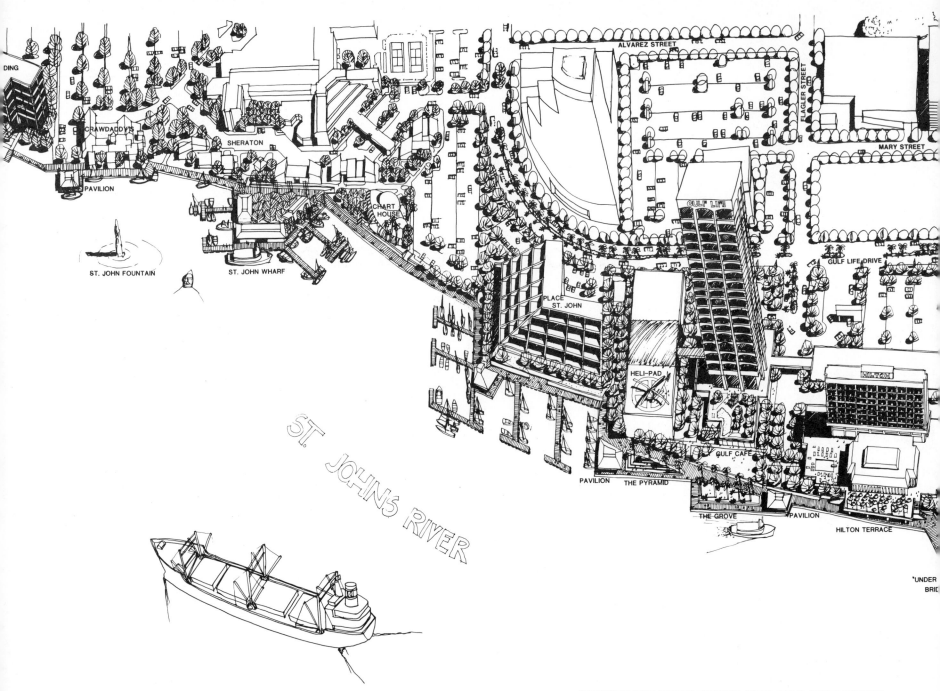

DING

CRAWDADDY'S

SHERATON

PAVILION

ST. JOHN FOUNTAIN

ST. JOHN WHARF

CHART HOUSE

ALVAREZ STREET

FLAGLER STREET

MARY STREET

GULF LIFE

PLACE ST. JOHN

GULF LIFE DRIVE

HELI-PAD

HILTON

GULF CAFÉ

PAVILION

THE PYRAMID

THE GROVE

PAVILION

HILTON TERRACE

ST. JOHNS RIVER

"UNDER
BRI

DOWNTOWN DEVELOPMENT AUTHORITY, SCOTT ADAMS, DEPUTY DIRECTOR

Waterfront Development

L. Azeo Torre

The illustration shows an aerial perspective site plan of a waterfront development with labels including:

FLEA MARKET, PRUDENTIAL, MARY STREET, DURAND STREET, SAN MARCO BLVD, GULF LIFE DRIVE, BANNER PROGRAM STREETS, SCIENCE MUSEUM, PARKING, DIAMONDHEAD RESTAURANT, ST. ALMO W ACOSTA BRIDGE, SCULPTURE, FRIENDSHIP PARK, VITA COURSE, HARBOR MASTER, SALT WATER, GREAT LAWN, AQUARIUM, FRESH WATER, FRIENDSHIP MARINA, AMPHITHEATRE, SHIP MUSEUM, WATER TAXI

VNR VAN NOSTRAND REINHOLD
New York

Printed in the United States of America

Van Nostrand Reinhold
115 Fifth Avenue
New York, New York 10003

Van Nostrand Reinhold (International) Limited
11 New Fetter Lane
London EC4P 4EE, England

Van Nostrand Reinhold
480 La Trobe Street
Melbourne, Victoria 3000, Australia

Macmillan of Canada
Division of Canada Publishing Corporation
164 Commander Boulevard
Agincourt, Ontario M1S 3C7, Canada

16 15 14 13 12 11 10 9 8 7 6
5 4 3 2 1

Library of Congress Cataloging in Publication Data

Torre, L. Azeo.
  Waterfront development/ L. Azeo Torre.
     p.   cm.
  Includes index.
  ISBN 0-442-21847-8
  1. Urban renewal—United States.
2. Waterfronts—United States.
3. City planning—United States.   I. Title.
HT175.T66 1989
307.1′4—dc19   88-20445
                                                  CIP

Cover: Southbank Riverwalk, Jacksonville, Florida.

Contents

Preface

All development responds to cycles. Just as the United States actively attempted to reestablish the life and viability of its cities' downtown centers during the 1970s, today a major new thrust is underway to reclaim those waterfronts from which the entire country grew. After turning our backs on these valuable assets for almost three to four decades and allowing industry and transportation to segregate us from life at the water's edge, we are now busy trying to restore not only what was there to begin with, but also to create even broader uses and activities that will contribute to and raise the overall quality and image of community life.

This book attempts to illustrate the unprecedented scale and breadth of current waterfront development. As the nation grows older and permits its citizens more recreational time than ever before, the consequent demand for the magical experience found at the water's edge is creating romantic projects for cities with populations of 10 thousand to 10 million. The shores of oceans, lakes, rivers, streams, and estuaries are all being explored and utilized to provide a fuller life experience for all people as well as educating them about their environment and world ecological and economic systems.

In researching development cycles, I found it instructive to look back at the state of waterfronts during different periods of history, at the shifting balance of quality of life and technological demands. Obviously, we are presently at the pinnacle of both, with an unprecedented demand for broader and greater recreational opportunities. In light of this, I found it most intriguing when my friend and colleague Max Conrad furnished a report by Frederick Law Olmsted, prepared in 1910 for the city of Pittsburgh for improvements to its waterfront. It reads:

At river ports throughout the world, the first primitive step, beyond the mere dumping of stuff and passengers on the natural shelving bank or river bed of mud or gravel, is the paving of the slope, as at Pittsburgh, still leaving the goods to be dragged up and down the bank by main force. But among the live modern river cities of Europe, wherever a real water competition with rail service has been desired, even though such competition be limited in its range, the day of the primitive or mud-bank type of shore has long gone by; and the public wharf has been reconstructed into one of the many well-recognized types of commercial embankment providing an up-to-date equipment for handling freight, and decent, attractive conditions for passengers. This development of the public wharf properties in Europe has kept pace with the activities of the railroads, making for the steady and intelligent improvement of terminal facilities. Indeed in many European river ports the impovement of the water terminals has rather forced the pace for the railroads.

In contrast to this active aggressive spirit, Pittsburgh, like most American river towns, where she has not actually turned her waterfront over bodily to the railroads, has left it in a most inefficient primitive condition.

But the value of Pittsburgh's waterfront lies not merely in its use as a wharf, however much improved. Another use, shown by the varied experiences of other river cities, is that, in a commercial waterfront on modern lines, there is generally opportunity for a wide marginal thoroughfare for the relief of traffic congestion in the adjacent streets. Sometimes such a waterfront throroughfare becomes a busy avenue of retail trade and general travel; but more usually its peculiar value lies in diverting some of the main streams of heavy teaming from the older interior streets where the retail trade and office business tend to concentrate, and where the passenger travel is most dense.

He concludes:

Wherever in the world, as an incident of the highways and wharves along its riverbanks, a city has provided opportunity for the people to walk and sit under pleasant conditions where they can watch the water and the life upon it, where they can enjoy the breadth of outlook and the sight of the open sky and the opposite bank and the reflections in the stream, the result has added to the comeliness of the city itself, the health and happiness of the people and their loyalty and local pride.

Of course Olmsted had no way of anticipating the future blossoming of festival market places, riverwalks, and similar concepts, which would add a new dimension to retail, commercial, and water-related activities. The success of these waterfront developments (in terms of both attendance and dollars per square foot), could not have been anticipated by anyone twenty years ago, let alone eighty years ago. But the basic anticipation of man's romance with the edge was.

With the tremendous waterfront resurgence that has occurred, a new consensus has evolved which knows no scale. Where only a decade ago it would have been extremely difficult to convince a community of 10,000 to 15,000

Top left: Biloxi's historic waterfront was based on the immediate working environment and integrated the shipbuiliding and seafood industries with recreation.

Bottom left: The development of Porto Cervo, Costa Smeralda. utilizes indigenous craftsmanship and subsequent vernacular to create a theme indicative of a waterfront culture.

people of the merits of a major capital expenditure to refurbish and animate their waterfront, today it is hard to find a community that is not in some phase of waterfront planning. This is why I have written this book.

Contained within these pages are some of the historic images that have influenced me and my firm, Cashio, Cochran, Torre/Design Consortium Ltd., our work, and our philosophy toward life at the water's edge. The examples given make up a patchwork quilt of different city sizes, locations, climates, and type of water area ranging from a man-made lake in Idaho to a prime location on the Hudson River in one of the largest cities in the world. Another notable aspect of all of these waterfronts is their financial success, coinciding with the explosion of the "business of recreation." Although open to every walk of life, economic level and interest, today's waterfronts can capitalize and operate on a self-sufficient basis and, in many cases, bring substantial economic development to the city. It is hoped that the reader will peruse, observe, and utilize these examples as well as others to develop an intuitive sense about the real potentials of their particular body of water's edge. It is at the edge that man is at his best, that life is its most vibrant and reiterative of the beauty and com-plexity of our adopted communal existence. This beauty can prevail in any geographic or climatic location, as it responds to the uniqueness of a site, a specific culture, or given economic structure, while connecting to historic and future global technologies. The reclamation of our greatest asset is only beginning. It is my hope that some of the following projects and principles will assist in improving future waterfronts as we return to the source.

Right: Portofino's waterfront in Italy, with its panoramic views and human-scale spaces and architecture, is one of the most successful developments in the world.

LIFE AT THE WATER'S EDGE

Water is the source of life that has both controlled and yet provided for human existence and all flora and fauna on earth. What starts in the rainforests and flows into the rivers of the world exudes a magic that no other element possesses. It is this artery that, while sustaining life, creates a unique environment and way of life at its edge. From the river to the lake, from the estuary to the ocean, the interaction of man and this edge has been the basis of a special relationship, one often characterized by potential danger but also by abundant rewards. The cosmopolitan richness and diversity of the world's port cities results from the desire to live at the edge despite impending weather crises and other catastrophies. New Orleans awaits the ultimate hurricane to inundate its leveed environment, which is 4 to 6 feet below sea level. San Francisco faces a potential seismic event that will transform a thriving metropolis of millions into an ocean floor. Meanwhile, Venice slowly sinks into the ground each year by fractions of an inch. But amid these and other impending events the cultures respond with an increased vibrancy of life, a desire to live for the moment. In Louisiana, the phrase *Le Bon Temps Roulé,* ("Let the Good Times Roll"), is a reiteration of a society that appreciates every moment of the life allowed at the water's edge. And what rewards that life brings. With its incredible bounty of the sea, it focus on various cultures and cuisine, it creates the basis for an ethnic diversity that repre-

Left: Fanning out into the bay, San Francisco's Pier 39 shows the successful adaptive reuse of a municipal pier into a properly scaled festival marketplace and working tourist waterfront.

sents the founding principle of the United States itself.

As a hub for every type of transportation, the city at the water's edge is bombarded constantly by a range of stimuli of foods, goods, systems, people, and vessels, requirements, and technologies such as bulkheads, sea walls, drainage, electrical, transporting devices, and the like. The development of an adequate response to these needs creates the development of a unique society, one which far more readily accepts change and, in fact, demands a greater diversity. This response creates a cohesive but broad-based culture.

But it is the lure of the water, its sparkle, its reflection, its endless movement and change, that both captures man's imagination and provides a variety of opportunities from business to recreation, from active to passive activities. It is perhaps because the United States is still a young nation that it has developed, then lost, and is presently redeveloping this edge that is so critical to its future well-being. The water's edge is where life is most diverse and unique. It is essential to human existence. Although the experience at this edge may exist at many

Top left: The Temple of Luxor maintains its magnificence today, 4,000 years after its construction at the edge of the Nile River.

Top right: Egyptian waterfront developers at an early morning sojourn at Luxor.

Bottom right: Modern day filuccas at work on the Nile vary little from their predecessors and remain the mainstay of this great river, providing services ranging from taxi to freighter.

scales, in different latitudes, and within varied geographic zones, it evokes the same magnetic response. It is at the water's edge that man is closest to the intuitive spirit that represents life itself.

Water has always been a conduit of technology. Even before the invention of the wheel, the Egyptians were able to build cities and monuments of colossal size by ferrying materials down river on barges. The water provided a medium which was, in essence, the only vehicle in this culture capable of carrying more weight than a camel. To successfully execute round trips, the fillucca (an Egyptian sailing vessel specifically adapted to the quiet waters of the Nile) was designed, a sailing vessel so perfect in design that it still sails the Nile's waters today.

THE PORT CITY

As refined versions of these sailing vessels ventured farther in pursuit of trade, specialization and adaptation continued to expand and to improve on the form of transportation, leading to great port cities that developed, in the Roman and Greek periods, for recreation, trade, and protection. Protection of the ports was vital due to the fact that one of the most effective ways for an invader to attack was en

Top left: The broad sidewalks along the Seine River in Paris offer recreational access to the waterfront.

Bottom left: Caglieri, Sardinia is a good example of the working waterfront, where industry, commerce, and recreation meet, creating an authentic experience.

Bottom right: Oxford, England makes the most of a tiny waterfront, with boat-rental, fishing, and swimming facilities, and linear parks.

masse by water as thousands of troops could be delivered quickly to the victim's door, weather permitting. Since the port settlement was located a substantial distance from the major city, however, it would take the enemy a day's march after arriving on shore before it could perpetrate an attack, offering protection for the victims.

This port city gave rise to a unique culture, with its diverse social environment. Reflecting the needs of many of the seamen who, after days at sea, rowdily pursued life's pleasures within set time limits, the port city developed a special intensity and life-style. Like the sea itself, the port city was constantly in a state of change, responding to weather, the introduction of many different cultures, the new technologies of the sea, and the subsequent rewards of more effective transportation and, therefore, greater trade and transportation, for better distribution of traded goods throughout new lands. As trade routes to the North American continent were established and various powers changed over time, the trade routes would eventually establish new founded port cities in the United States; these cities reflected a heritage and a unique flavor from which they would grow.

Top right: Piazza San Marco exemplifies a waterfront development that is oriented successfully toward the water although it has very little direct access to it. An important feature is the width of the waterfront promenade—in excess of 50 feet.

Bottom right: A city divided by its river, Florence manages to make the link with the Ponte Vecchio, a bridge lined with shops and activities, initiating what has become known today as the "festival marketplace."

THE AMERICAN PORT CITY

The early port cities that developed in the United States were virtually identical to their European counterparts. With the arrival of the Industrial Revolution and the railroads, however, both the scale and image of the cities changed dramatically. Initially, American port cities were the first points of arrival and centers for social interaction and entertainment. As commerce increased, the requirements for storage and movement grew, and port cities actually cut off their inhabitants from access to the water's edge with vast warehouses, rail spurs, wharves, and arterials that provided for the distribution of goods. With the introduction of the automobile, waterfront access was curtailed even further—where once was a promenade for strolling amid fish markets and harbors filled with ships from around the world, became an expressway, generally elevated, to connect one side of the port city to the other. It is unfortunate that the dream for growth and prosperity caused so many icons of the United States maritime legacy to become lost before American society reached a high level of maturity and sophistication to demand access to their greatest asset, the water's edge. Within the last twenty years, there has been an incredible resurgence of interest in reclaiming and enjoying this magical zone in all its varied sizes, both large and small city and water body sizes.

Top left: At the turn of the century the New Orleans riverfront was alive with activity and accessible to the public. Until recently, in the twentieth century, however, access was provided only at the Moonwalk *(bottom left)* a 300-foot-long boardwalk at the Mississippi River's edge.

REDISCOVERING AN OLD ASSET

Major waterfront development has occurred primarily within the last decade, as the public has begun to demand its port areas back. Revitalization has ranged from New York to Pascagoula, Mississippi, based on this relatively recent, 1970s, desire to work, play, and live at the water's edge. The original innovators— like Boston, Baltimore, Seattle, San Francisco,—have shown other cities the way. Millions of tourists have joined local inhabitants in getting back to the water's edge, providing the basis for a new positive economic impact on the community. But the resurgence of waterfront appreciation has gone even further than the original precedents' breadth of development in terms of use and, particularly, scale. Whereas it would have been very difficult at the turn of the century to package a waterfront development for a city of 30,000 inhabitants, it is actually feasible to do so today. There is no other place like the water's edge. As a result, contemporary society has developed a consensus that has created the basis for this return.

Top left: With a long maritime history, San Francisco's Fisherman's Wharf was the first of its genre, dealing with waterfront image, public access and use.

Top right: South Street Seaport in New York provides a link to the city's seafaring history as well as to the river from which it grew.

Bottom right: The bridges of Port Grimaud, France provide both image and access within this waterfront community.

RECLAIMING THE WATERFRONT

The return to the water's edge is not an easy one and usually involves a myriad of problems, ranging from riparian rights of adjacent property owners to public perception of the value of public space. In other words, if the waterfront has been lucky enough to have avoided the construction of an expressway along its edge, separating it from the rest of the city, then it is probably perceived as the adjacent landowners' personal property for their private use. This, along with other land-use and zoning issues, liability, security, access and circulation, is a problem that must be dealt with to provide focus on the asset of the water for recreational purposes, rather than these issues being parasitic to only the water's industrial requisites (solely for transportation purposes).

Left: The variety of bridges in Amsterdam, Holland create a unique image and theme for the city.

Bottom right: Since the city of New Orleans is located below sea level, the surrounding levees provide flood protection as well as recreation.

The desire to reclaim the waterfront must be created or supported by the entire community in order to solve these problems. Whether through public forum, political process, private initiative, or a combination of all three, the water's edge can be recaptured. It is important to remember that the underpinning of a successful waterfront is the formation of a consensus. Waterfront development is, fortunately, an emotional issue for which a consensus can be easily established based on the merits of a particular project. The real challenge is in balancing the elements of the consensus so as to move in a unified direction and to avoid in-fighting as the project goes from the broad-brush planning stage to the detailed land-use and design drawings that will ultimately create the waterfront's character.

PRINCIPLES OF WATERFRONT DEVELOPMENT TO THE NEW PROCESSES

The political and economic dynamics that were responsible for the waterfronts of the past are as dissimilar to today's processes as are oil and water. Although an intriguing, old abandoned wharf may have a would-be waterfront developer thinking of potential uses ranging from an aquarium to a museum to a restaurant and shopping area, there are usually those with different ideas. Thus, it is useful to

Top right: The fountains of the Jardins du Trocadero create a spectacular linkage to the Seine River and the Eiffel Tower.

Bottom right: A small waterway community in Stockholm, Sweden combines residential and industrial vessels. The trees provide a backdrop and give a sense of enclosure to the environment.

start with the basic concept that the waterfront is a melting pot of issues and interests: the key word in development is *compromise.* Obviously, it is impossible to occupy every square foot of waterfront space with "people places" and "festival market places" (special themed retail developments) because not all such spaces will be used continually and because of the requirements of a diversified economy. Establishing a successful balance of uses will enable all facilities or uses under consideration to be realized to at least some degree, to come to life, and to avoid the death of a waterfront project because of disagreement. Working out all the issues also allows for a greater diversity in expression on the water's edge and therefore actually creates a stronger base for repeated visitor attendance. The opportunity to dine on the water's edge while watching a working port in action creates an exciting backdrop to the waterfront experience for the user. The traffic of different ships and cargoes serves to both educate the visitor and to underline the international flavor of the experience and perhaps the cuisine. We refer to these nodal zones, points of internal or focused activity, as "windows" on the river, lake, or stream. These "windows," if successfully implemented, allow for the coexistence of multiple land uses while providing authenticity (not, for example, an amusement park, but a real, working

Top left: On the Grand Canal in Venice, the Rialto Bridge serves image and function with its internal marketplace.

Bottom left: The pleasure piers of Brighton, England are as exciting today as when they were first built, hosting millions of visitors each year.

waterfront) to the waterfront development theme.

On the smaller-scale lake or creek, a development can potentially unite water-oriented recreational activities such as swimming, rowing, and water-skiing with adjacent amenities, such as restrooms, ramps, parks, and residential or commercial facilities. The definition of uses is as broad as the conception of a given project —based on demographics, theme, economics, and public perception. The basic principle in creating and taking advantage of these amenities is balancing public response and participation, for it will be their attachment to and attendance at the development that will allow it to live or die. The most important goal in developing the waterfront is to achieve this balance.

Top left: A dinghy serves as vehicle to the yachts in the Portofino basin.

Bottom left: Pier 39 San Francisco features a dramatic entry that draws visitors into a space in which the architecture is sheathed with the siding from the former wharf structure.

Bottom right: At Expo '82 in Knoxville, Tennessee the central water feature's edge was variously articulated to provide for many uses.

HISTORIC
WATERFRONTS

There are literally thousands of incredible waterfronts around the world. All are based on the same principles and function, although they operate within different geographic zones and different cultures. The following examples show some of the possibilities of the scale, shape, and volume for potential projects. Although they do not represent a comprehensive collection of all the great waterfronts, they have served as models for many contemporary waterfronts and, for countless people throughout history, have been considered some of the most romantic places in the world.

The romantic waterfronts of Italy combine working harbors, resort facilities, public beaches, and commercial centers in a way that always seems to be balanced in terms of scale and function, no matter what the back-up demographics (economics, population earnings, jobs, costs, etc.) might be. Among the numerous ports, Positano, Amalfi and their surrounding coastal regions offer incredible hill towns that spill down the steep mountainside to azure waters and pebble beaches. Positano is clearly one of the most beautiful among Italian port towns, with a composite architecture facade, different architectural styles, patch-quilted together, based largely on the Moorish vault. The joint use of the roofs of houses as terraces for the living quarters above represents one of the fundamentals of waterfront developments, that is, getting multiple use of each element. The warmth of the stuccoed walls and tile roofs completes the visual image and the setting. The severity of the Amalfi Peninisula slope prevents automobiles from reaching the lower levels of the city, making the visitor's experience increasingly pedestrian the closer he gets to the water. Commercial uses are woven into the meandering street scenes, forcing the visitor to "evolve" from one area to another. At the beach level, the early morning is occupied

Bottom left: In Positano, the principles of multiple use are clearly displayed. The brightly colored working fishermen's boats use the swimming beach along with tourists and set an effective backdrop for them. *Bottom right:* The architecture clings to the mountain edge, using the roof of each lower residential unit to serve as the balcony for the unit above.

by the activities of the fishermen and their boats, slowing toward midday as tourists enjoy the beach, rent boats, swim, and the restaurants begin to open. This scene continues into the night. The tourist and fisherman exist side by side, recreating and working, which gives the waterfront experience its authenticity. The visitor is in awe of the geographic surroundings and at the same time engulfed in the romantic image of man and the sea. Water is both the thematic backdrop and the major land use for transportation, circulation, life support, and the like.

To Venice, the water goes beyond this to the end that it is the basic concept. Water is no longer the edge but the arterial. From the vaporetti (water buses) to the garbage and concrete-mixer boats, all important daily activity is conducted via water. Because the city is located on a lagoon, without waves or tidal fluctuation, every edge of the land is easily accessible. All land uses externalize themselves to the liquid arterials. Bridges become sculptural edifices for land use, like the Ponte Rialto, one of the original "festival market places" (a speciality retail waterfront themed development with shops, restaurants, and the like. The term was coined by Rouse's Boston waterfront development, Faneuil Hall). The water's function as conduit for bus, taxis, industry, commerce, and recreational vessels is turned to theatrical purposes, with activities such as the Regatta Storica, a parade of histori-

Top right: The Grand Canal in Venice serves as both the main street and the vehicular conduit of this island/city.

Bottom right: The Grand Canal becomes a stage through which the parade vessels pass during the Regatta Storica.

cal vessels. This celebration has translated into similar events throughout the world under numerous names such as Blessing of the Fleet and Christmas Water Parade. Every sidewalk, no matter how small, becomes a mini plaza lined with covered tables. No matter what the size of the restaurant, shop, or market, the scale is uncharacteristically the same, and through function, creates the tactile waterfront experience (one can touch it and put one's toes in it as opposed to merely viewing it from behind a rail).

Florence demonstrates a response to different criteria. With the Arno River flowing through its core, which is radically affected by runoff and subsequent floodwater levels, the city's waterfront experience is basically of a view of the river over a stone parapet to a battered stone wall below. Florence's great bridge, the Ponte Vecchio, broadens this experience while linking two sides of the city, like Venice's Rialto. The articulated facade of the covered bridge delineates the diversity of stores and shops within, allowing the visitor to experience the Arno River other than from its austere protective edge. But a limiting factor to waterfront development is a practical response to catastrophic events. The walls that protect the city from floodwaters also separate it from heavy recreational use of the river.

Top left: Aqua Alta extends Venice's waterfront into Piazza San Marco during high winter tides.

Bottom left: The Ponte Vecchio in Florence, Italy wears city fabric from both sides of the Arno river, providing cohesion along a riverfront devoid of recreational amenities.

Facing page, bottom left: A neighborhood scene on one side of the interior canals of Venice serves as a perfect delineation of scale.

The Ponte Vecchio attempts to mitigate this circumstance in a unique cultural way through applying multiple use to function.

Rome, on the other hand, maintains very little rapport with the Tiber River. Once a navigable waterway that provided limited trade and commerce to and from Rome, the river today represents only a visual asset. At the bottom of its white stone walls is a walkway that permits the pedestrian to get close to the water's edge at low water; however, access is extremely limited and difficult because of a steep ramp and steps. Perhaps it is because this incredible city has turned toward its plethora of piazzas for respite that it has felt no real need to attempt to reunite its development with the artery that brought it life. Nonetheless, as a thematic element, the river affords a spectacular backdrop.

Top right: Author and son Azeo attempt to make contact with the Tiber River's edge in Rome—unsuccessfully. *Bottom right:* Although the water is devoid of acceptable access, the trees along the edge provide much-needed shade and help mitigate adjacent automobile noise and pollution.

The Seine in Paris offers a very different kind of waterfront. As a major navigable waterway, it is host not only to commerce and industry but also to residential and recreational uses. With many barges and boats at its edge and glorious bridges with cafés adjacent, it is the center of city life. Active and interesting, changing in both scale and function, the Seine becomes the conduit of visitor experience. An interesting recent event was the artist Christo's wrapping of the Pont Neuf, which drew crowds of delighted visitors.

Top left and *bottom right:* Christo's wrapping of the Pont Neuf created a major event in Paris, bringing hundreds of thousands of people out to celebrate at the water's edge. *Bottom left:* The Seine affords good riverfront access to the pedestrian and a dramatic progression toward Christo's sculpture.

The sculptural wrapping of the bridge exemplifies the importance of events in waterfront developments, in which public attendance brings greatly increased use of adjacent cafés, shops, and restaurants.

Amsterdam provides a critical lesson in scale. Its canals are for the most part very small, yet highly utilized. Adequate walkways, buildings of proper scale (four to six stories), and substantial tree plantings create the same kind of ambience and waterfront experience in a northern latitude that can be found at Mediterranean ports. All the elements work together, from the iron railings on bridges to the intricate stone plazas that open up the city fabric to the water edge. Commercial and residential uses coexist successfully with multi-leveled placement of buildings and facilities and strict sign control. It is this layering, again, that underpins the multiple-use concept.

In Istanbul, with its floating bridges, it is possible not only to dine or have tea or coffee on a bridge itself but also to be able to buy fresh fried seafood cooked and served directly from the boat by the fisherman who caught it from the dock alongside the bridge. Autos drive overhead, while pedestrians and a complex array of related land uses exist below the bridge structure. This approach is one that has

Left: Amsterdam's scale, architecture, street trees, signage, and working waterfront make it one of Europe's most livable northern-latitude cities.

Top right: Fried fish can be purchased hot from the boat and the fisherman's frying pan on the Istanbul waterfront.

Bottom right: Dubrovnik exists as a complex, detailed urban fabric within medieval walls, with a small port (seen at right).

hardly been explored, especially in the United States, with the exception of the River Café at the base of the Brooklyn Bridge in New York. What seems to be constantly undervalued is the value of the waterfront setting in terms of its views, location, and romance.

Often criticized by archaeologists for its overdone restoration, Dubrovnik, Yugoslavia is a classic in terms of *le tout ensemble,* or its complete sense of place.

The walled city, inland or coastal, starts with a greater fabric geometry (exterior shape) and less amorphism than most cities. Dubrovnik's design establishes a singular image while creating a variety of space and nooks that both inhabitants and tourists can explore. Its harbor is small, which reflects its internalized land uses because of storm protection (by i.e., walls, bulkheads, etc.), in contrast to that of Positano for example.

One of the smallest, yet most effective waterfronts is that of the Plaza de Spaña in Seville, Spain. The formal plaza, built for the 1929 Spanish/American Exhibition, rich in detail and materials, offers a semi-circular moat at its edge, which is heavily used for recreational boating. Although small and undersized for any real boating activity, it establishes a theme of play and transforms a formal lagoon into a site for fun. Additionally, it proves that there are no rules as to scale and function if innovation prevails.

If Portofino is the prima donna of the small, romantic ports of Italy, Hilton Head Island, South Carolina is certainly its counterpart in the United States. Its scale (three to four levels) and function (multiple use) are reiterative of Mediterranean port towns. The water's edge combines public spaces, restaurants, and marina facilities with parklike environments. The marina shape is more pretty than functional, but, nonetheless, it is the effective foundation of *le tout ensemble*.

A lesson learned well from the European waterfronts is that of image. The brightly striped lighthouse is more image than function, but it creates a highly distinguishable image for the Hilton Head development in the United States and also internationally. The towns and villages of Martha's Vineyard have followed this approach in a more ad hoc manner, giving clarity of image to a total island waterfront development without having to identify any particular element.

Top left: Plaza de Spaña in Seville, Spain offers waterfront recreation by means of a fountain pool 25 feet in width.

Bottom left: The terraces of Isola Bella on Lago Maggiore in Italy provide a grand layering of uses, culminating at the palace above.

Top right: Hilton Head, South Carolina reiterates its Italian counterpart, Portfino.

Center right: Its image-making lighthouse is shown here with dramatic night lighting.

Bottom right: Martha's Vineyard offers a much less intense development, providing more for country squireship.

Top and *bottom left:* The sweeping radius of Portofino's moorage allows a logical separation of larger vessels to the outside and smaller yachts to the inside beside the bulkhead. The terminus of the harbor is a ramp from which the workboats are launched. The entire harbor is surrounded by shops, restaurants, and commercial facilities with residences above.

The main street in Isla Mujeres, Mexico, creates an image that is conducive to recreation while at the same time representing a working waterfront. The waterfront docks are places both to play and to work —to unload cargo or to charter a boat for snorkeling. Unlike its sister waterfronts of Cancún and Cozumel, Isla Mujeres is purported to be the locals' vacation spot. With the authenticity and romantic flavor of its waterfront, shops, and restaurants, it is truly an oasis in the Gulf of Mexico and has recently finally developed a full-service marina, which accommodates yachtsmen from around the world. Full-service facilities are crucial for any development in that the availability of security, lighting, communications, and lodging, among other provisions, which make a development an international magnet as opposed to a regional waterfront. The opportunity to plan a gulf crossing of one week and leave the vessel in a protected area for some time prior to returning to home port increases visitorship and makes the development competitive with other premier recreation destinations.

In the United States yachting is a major underpinning use that sustains land use in waterfront development. The American east and west coasts have shown the most direct response to the technology (e.g., systems, decking, electrical, seawalls) required to effectively package these facilities. The Gulf of Mexico is sorely in need of facilities, with marina slip shortages from Texas to Florida probably exceeding 7,000 slips.

Top and bottom left: The working waterfront of Isla Mujeres ranges from bustling activity at the public dock to serene tranquility on the leeward side of the island, sheltered from the tradewinds.

Although reportedly one of the largest marina facilities in the world, Marina del Rey in Los Angeles effectively serves the boating community in terms of technical requirements but offers little in terms of image and romance. No evidence exists of any consideration of historic precedents, leaving the overall development somewhat characterless, even though the facility is both successful and technically proficient. Marinas are villages and thus must be secure, reviewing their development plus life, and capable of maintaining privacy. Those who supply the boats that provide the backdrop to hundreds of land uses essentially "live" in the marina, so that both availability of services and autonomy need to prevail. The multiple-use concept is not externalized sufficiently at Marina del Rey and subsequently no landside "village" has been created. Even greater departures from the village scheme have been put into place in Battery Park City, New York, where for thousands of feet of adjacent multistory buildings, a small marina of less than one hundred slips is available. The village marina has not been allowed to develop because of lack of privacy and scale.

Bahia Mar in Fort Lauderdale, Florida, offers an adequate marina with good access to the intracoastal waterway canal and the Atlantic Ocean but is not complete as a waterfront community since it lacks the residential element. This is a common approach used in the past to provide services and slips for the boating community while falling short of creating

Top and bottom right: Marina City presents a hard, cold, and unromantic image of a waterfront although it does offer a full-service marina facility.

the landside village needed to establish the development.

John's Pass in Saint Petersburg, Florida offers less for the marina user and more for the visitor in a small-scale development of boardwalks, shops, one restaurant, and the backdrop of a working harbor. It is user friendly and unpretentious, allowing the visitor to feel at ease. It "feels" authentic and, created on a low budget, offers a very different model of the festival marketplace from that exemplified by the Rouse Company developments.

The Rouse Company, Columbia, Maryland (land developer and creator of the Festival Marketplace concept) has become the waterfront-development guru of larger American cities, among them Baltimore and Boston. South Street Seaport in New York, also designed by Rouse Company, is successful in terms of its overall scale, architecture, and the breadth of adjacent activities. Although development may have meant the loss of the "real" sea-

Top left: Bahia Mar in Fort Lauderdale provides a comprehensive marina facility but little for visitors with the flavor of the city's history.

Bottom left: Boston's Faneuil Hall serves as an integral part of the entire waterfront although it is located fairly far from the water's edge.

Top, center, and bottom right: John's Pass in Saint Petersburg, Florida delineates an enjoyable, funky waterfront development composed almost entirely of "joints."

Facing page, bottom left: South Street Seaport, New York.

Facing page, top right: The *USS Constellation* moored in front of the Rouse Festival Marketplace complex.

Facing page, bottom right: On board the *Constellation,* one is able to have a tactile experience of Baltimore's historic waterfront.

food shops (where one could have a plate of steamers while fish were being cleaned in the background) the overall renewal provided *more,* renovated important formerly forgotten city fabric, and provided a ship museum and event center, which reattaches sailing history to the New York waterfront.

A different kind of waterfront is the internal body of water created for a special purpose. Following the concept of the Plaza de España in Seville, the creators of Expo '82 took downtown railroads in Knoxville, Tennessee and transformed them, for six months, into a water garden. The fair could not have been successful in the middle of summer without the visual and psychological effects of this concourse. Ironically, the fabricated waterfront of Expo '82 was far more successful and offered more to the visitor than did Expo '84 in New Orleans, even though the 1984 site was located directly on the Mississippi River. Much of New Orleans' problem concerned the fair visitors' separation from the water's edge because of navigational hazards, flood levels, port ac-

Top left and bottom right: Without this central watercourse at Knoxville's Expo '82, the summer heat would have been unbearable.

tivities, and existing bulkheads. Whereas the Knoxville design allowed the visitor to dangle his feet in the water, the ill-fated New Orleans fair used the Mississippi River as a backdrop only, with the visitor set back ten feet from the edge and twenty feet in elevation above it. The technical issue of making the pedestrian link to the edge is a major challenge that must be successfully resolved if the waterfront development is to come to life.

Center left: New Orleans' Expo '84 created very little linkage to the Mississippi River, using it primarily as a backdrop, one of the downfalls of the design.

Top and bottom right: Tivoli Gardens in Copenhagen provides a recreational waterfront in the middle of the city with man-made thematic waterways.

On a small scale reminiscent of Amsterdam, San Antonio's waterfront shows the linkage and theming of a very narrow water concourse into a major land-use development. Barges rented for events or evening dining create an atmosphere of entertainment and enjoyment. Again, the romantic bridge element connects both sides of the city while creating an image, allowing the visitor to become completely involved with the development's edges and land uses.

These are only a few of the waterfronts that range in size and scale from oceanfront to river, from lagoon to pond. But no matter what their scale, all respond to the basic desire of most people to be near the water's edge. People want a cozy, unique place to sit, drink, dine, walk, and people-watch, amid the sound, sparkle, and movement of water.

A total development needs to have a life of its own before it can effectively offer experiences to visitors from outside its own boundaries.

Its economic stability should be based on its complexity of multiple-use functions. Its theme should be proper and authentic, not contrived. The image should respond to the romantic, and it must be technically proficient in response to tide, height of wave created, and storm protection. But, above all, it must be both seen and accessible to everyone at all levels.

Top left: San Antonio's Riverwalk provides a comprehensive series of recreational resources along a very narrow drainage canal.

Bottom left: The pleasure piers of Brighton take the waterfront visitor away from the edge and into the ocean environment.

Top left: Heidelberg's riverfront, lined with plazas and promenades planted with trees, is a reiteration of the city's love of walking.

Bottom left and top right: A riverfront development achieves success if its components are properly linked and styled, as is the case of Cologne, Germany's Rhine River waterfront.

Center right: The marina is a village that must offer flexibility of use, privacy, comfort, full service, and accommodation of a full range of vessel sizes.

ELEMENTS OF A
SUCCESSFUL PROJECT

THEME

Perhaps nothing is as important to the development's future as effectively searching out its history. Establishing a successful theme will control future spatial analysis, land-use materials, scale, and meaning. Frequently, initial stages of design are referred to as "thematic" rather than schematic. It is at these stages that the project's romantic aspect will or will not be realized.

The theme is determined by several factors. Response to climate is the first consideration. The layout, design, and land use of a development in a cold, northern region will be quite different from that of one located in a southern area, although the basic functions will be the same. Delineating the special element(s) about that specific project's culture and history is another factor. Establish a reason for people to return to the water's edge showing them potential uses in a very personal way.

Facing page, top left: West End in New Orleans, circa 1901, uses Amsterdam-like bridge and galleried architecture. *Facing page, bottom left:* Brighton Pleasure Piers' collage of similar turrets, overlooks, and towers within a different vernacular.

Top left: Hilton Head's mock lighthouse has become its image and logo, delineating the importance of the image.

Top right: Expo '82 articulated its theme of energy with a central watercourse featuring a high-technology windmill.

Center left: The Hotel Medina, on the Isle of D'Jerba, Tunisia, utilizes the image and function of indigenous barrel-vault architecture to weave a complex and unique village fabric.

Bottom right: Rock Creek in Washington, D.C. provides a link to the city's historic waterway system, with barges still towed by mules.

Top right: The re-use of a submarine base in Saint Thomas in the American Virgin Islands creates a wonderful scale and introduction to shops and restaurants.

Top left: In Frankfurt, Germany a residential development implies a water orientation but denies the inhabitants direct access to the amenity's edge.

Bottom left: The urban landscape of Chicago is softened by the pastoral waterfront edge.

Facing page, bottom right: Positano demonstrates the drama of multiple use and layering of facilities. The backdrop to the first level back is the location of shops and restaurants.

Facing page, top: In West End, in New Orleans, circa 1901, the architecture is logical for the climate with galleries, natural ventilation, and orientation. A barge delivers freshly cut cypress logs to the center of the city via the New Basin Canal.

Facing page, bottom left: In West End, in New Orleans, circa 1986, not only has the richness and texture of the waterfront been lost, but standards of quality for most of the facilities' operations have also disappeared. (The right-of-way in the background is the filled-in New Basin Canal.)

IMAGE

Developing a broad range of ways to respond to a wealth of desired activities, from boating to sitting and people watching, is important. Will visitors sit on an iron or wooden bench? Should furnishings be contemporary or historic? Research should provide the theme; the assemblage and materials should create the image.

The image gives the visitor perception of the project before coming to the waterfront and forming an opinion. If a devel-

Top left: Unfortunately there are too few contemporary waterfront designs that have been successfully, and romantically, designed. Marina City, California and the sculptural pie-slice condominiums *(top right)* on the island of Sardinia, Italy, fall far short of the communal habitat of Port Grimaud, France *(bottom left).*

Bottom right: The complex patterns of street paving in Amsterdam show the importance of rich materials toward the creation of image.

oper is successful, both the developer and the client should walk away with the same idea. Many of the waterfront development images to date have become standards. A Rouse waterfront development can be identified immediately by its standing seam-metal roof and building shapes. This is not bad in itself, but there are so many cities seeking to replicate Rouse's success that they are reproducing the image verbatim. Every waterfront needs its own theme and image to be unique.

AUTHENTICITY

A waterfront that is alive with water-dependent activities is the basis for an authentic and enjoyable experience. Long looked upon as negative, adjacent industrial functions can offer interest and education to the visitor. A waterfront restaurant in San Francisco, for example,

Bottom left: Mont Saint Michel daily mantains the unique distinction of being both a landlocked walled city and a waterfront island daily, because of bay tides.

Top and *bottom right:* The tiny city of Bosa in Sardinia demonstrates the simplicity and success of an authentic waterfront fishing community. The function creates the setting, and tourist visitation logically follows.

announces the name, tonnage, cargo, and port of origin of each vessel passing by, bringing the excitement of far-off lands to the dining experience.

FUNCTION

No matter how unique or exciting a waterfront development is, it will be a success only if it functions well on all levels. From regional access and circulation to adequate parking capacity, to ease and comfort of pedestrian movement, to the visitors' overall experience, all levels must sequence successfully, as well as meet capacities on peak activity days.

Local codes, of course, control many of these aspects in terms of parking spaces per square foot of development, walkway widths, and so on. But it is important to look for ways to provide the necessary spatial envelope while creating a total environment with multiple-use capabilities. The plaza that can be used for concerts may have access steps that can be used as an amphitheater. Or, a gathering area might be able to accommodate a farmer's or fisherman's market in the morning, a flower boutique in the afternoon, and a concert at night. Campo de Fiore in Rome functions much like this, with eating establishments interspersed between various commercial activities throughout the day.

Opportunities to eat, people-watch, or simply sit and relax are essential to a suc-

Top left: Although nowhere near the water's edge, the Tuilleries in Paris provide shade, rest, and food along the route to the Seine.

Bottom left: The riverfront along the Thames River in London is about as inviting as the weather. Note the benches are awkwardly placed, elevated on pedestals to allow views above the overly heavy handrail.

cessful waterfront development. The shops and commercial facilities will be only as successful as the "free" experience component is outside. Programming for these outside areas is also crucial. From mimes to music, fireworks to laser displays, the waterfront should be programmed for daily events, with attention given to planning for special events and holidays—blessings of the fleet, waterfront festivals, seafood festivals and so on. These events draw more people to the water's edge and create a greater awareness of this special environment and a city's cultural legacy.

PUBLIC PERCEPTION OF NEED; FORMING A CONSENSUS

To form a consensus, a potential developer must "sell" his or her idea to the majority. Carefully formulated, well thought-out plans that effectively respond to theme, image, authenticity, function, and financial and environmental concerns must be brought before interested citizens in public meetings. The developer must be open to the ideas and feedback from these sessions, which will help him to anticipate what will be acceptable and what will not. It is important to come up with fallback options to understand clearly how to phase the development if necessary. The developer must understand what "core" elements must be realized successfully within the total project. Most waterfront development will involve some, if not a major part, of public land in

Top right: Bayshore Boulevard is transformed from a scenic drive and linear park development to event center *(bottom right)* during the Gasparilla Day Festival where the City of Tampa is invaded by modern-day pirates in a celebration of maritime heritage.

TAMPA TRIBUNE—BAYSHORE AERIAL PHOTOS/PHOTO LAB

its acreage. Changing the use of that land, —whether a trash heap or playground— to another use will be evaluated on the basis of protecting the public trust. The change must be for the good of all.

Riparian rights, (the ownership rights to the water's edge) of the adjacent landowners surely will arise at some point. In many cases, roadways or public lands were built out in front of the original parcels of land as transportation improvements. The problem arises when the waterfront development attempts to bring in more people from the region or promote increased activity and the owner of the adjacent land attempts to restrict views or access. The developer should be prepared to take this matter to court.

Legal liability and the instigation of lawsuits have become unfortunately popular. This has forced many municipal, state, and federal facilities to cut back on bringing people to the water's edge, because of the chance of a visitor's slipping on wet surface or falling in the water and drowning; flooding, and so on. Waterfront developments are being tested constantly through litigation. Tort reform may resolve many of these problems, but the architects and designers for these developments need to take into account that the water's edge has and always will be a potentially hazardous zone.

FINANCIAL FEASIBILITY

If any land use development can succeed in a city, then a waterfront development is feasible. There is nothing comparable to a successful waterfront development, if effectively packaged, designed, promoted, managed and operated. However, the development must be sound in its understanding of demographics, community buying power, response to the project, and future prospects. Once a substantial concept is developed, it should be tested financially to establish size, magnitude, and public response. A large community will probably look to one of the "big eight" accounting firms for this task; a smaller area can be successful with local economists who have an understanding of community "pulse." In many cases, the local Chamber of Commerce can furnish the developer with enough profile data to begin to assess project parameters.

The first step should be to examine the basic opportunities that exist at the waterfront. This should not take a tremendous amount of research but it is essential to determine whether or not there are enough boat slips or full-service marinas or places to eat on the waterfront and what the potential is for adequate access to and programming of the waterfront as a resource. If the basic opportunities

exist, the developer can proceed to the feasibility stage after developing the thematic plan. It is important that the concept lead the financial assessment, and not the reverse.

ENVIRONMENTAL APPROVALS

The permit process for waterfront development has become increasingly difficult. The wetland laws have effectively protected estuaries against the rampant filling and bulkheading projects of the 1950s and 1960s. The problem, however, is that the present processes are extremely slow and involve many steps. The developer must obtain approvals from many individual agencies, including the Corps of Engineers (COE), the Environmental Protection Agency (EPA), the U.S. Fish and Wildlife Service (FWS), the U.S. National

Marine Fisheries Services (NMFS), the Departments of Archives and History, Marine Resources, Pollution Control, and Storm Water. A recent development in permit-granting for larger projects has been the creation of a Special Management Area (SMA) whose purpose is to bring all these agencies together to determine environmental impact, mitigation, and project feasibility at one time. Inter-agency meetings can formulate a consensus of what is allowable under permit, avoiding the problem of a proposal that is granted a permit by one agency but not by another.

In any case, the environmental review process must be started early, as the time and effort it takes to establish a mitigation plan will severely affect the feasibility of a project if not planned for in advance. The developer must be open, research the ecological processes of the project area,

Facing page, top left: Marinas must offer full services and effective designs to compete for the attention of and achieve local and regional success with yachtsmen.

Facing page, bottom left: The most popular element that has appeared recently on the waterfront is the aquarium. Purported to be the most successful such facility in the United States, the Monterey Aquarium has gone far beyond self-sufficient operation to realize millions of dollars in profit.

Bottom right: The importance of impact on estuary and coastal zone systems must be realized and effectively dealt with in a successfully developed waterfront. These areas are the richest and most beautiful centers of life on earth and should steer the design, not fall victim to it.

design to mitigate impacts, and utilize the development site's resources in a logical and conscientious way. A rule of thumb is that for every acre of impact the developer must provide two acres of mitigation, and, for the most part, enhancement does not count. Designers should always remember that a waterfront development pursued without obtaining the proper permits is punishable by law. The port director of a recent development received several days in jail and a heavy fine for attempting to backfill a marsh.

CONSTRUCTION TECHNOLOGY

No matter where the waterfront development is located, one of the major tasks will be to stabilize the edge where land and water meet. This battle for stabilization has been on going since man first sought to develop and create life directly at the water's edge. Traditional techniques ranged from setting stones in either breakwater or riprap fashion, to the later more economical use of timber. Steel-sheet pile is a relatively new material in this stabilization effort, spanning less than seventy-five years. The introduction of prestressed and precast concrete sheet piling in sandy- or softer bottomed bodies of water, created a long-lived system capable of responding to major storms, but established basis for the $1,500 to $2,000

Top left: Stability is based on complexity, and barrier islands are great examples of principles of nature. The dunes, plantings, and fauna allow for flexibility but can withstand the onslaught of the inevitable storm.

Bottom left: Contemporary marina design utilizes many systems for moorage. Pier 39 elected to use a floating-dock system instead of a fixed pier because of water depth.

per linear foot cost that exists today. Even a wooden system will cost $200 to $400 per linear foot, and its life span is probably no more than thirty to forty years. As these bulkheads, breakwaters, and jetties are a prerequisite for stabilization of the water's edge and since this reinforcement produces no revenue, its cost must be defrayed by adjacent land uses. It is imperative to use the most long-lived, cost-effective system available for a specific zone.

A system that has been used with great success was developed in Italy with installations as early as 1894. Gabions,—wire boxes filled with different-sized stones—are tied together and stacked like huge stones. The image is effective and architectural, but the real beauty is the price. A comparable concrete-sheet pile system, which would cost $2,000 per foot, can be achieved in gabions for as little as $400 per linear foot, with a life span of up to sixty years in salt water with the new Polyvinyl chloride coatings. An additional benefit is the gabion's ability to function as a reef or habitat, a major environmental benefit.

Top right: The gabion bulkhead/seawall system provides effective stabilization at the water's edge while enhancing the habitat with its shelf-like construction—all at one-quarter of the cost of conventional sheet-pile bulkheading.

Bottom right: The ultimate disposition of a wooden sheet-pile bulkhead.

Bottom left: Bahia Mar in Fort Lauderdale effectively utilizes prepackaged electrical service systems, proper dockage walkways, dock boxes, and other facilities necessary to effectively serve the yachtsman. The striking harbor master building serves as the development's image maker, much like the lighthouse at Hilton Head in South Carolina.

In terms of electrical and mechanical systems, many prepackaged types respond to marina and waterfront facility needs. These are, in many cases, presealed or have coatings that will allow them to withstand the considerable effects of corrosion in waterfront environments. For metal parts, there is no substitute for stainless steel: its high initial cost is quickly made up for in ease of short- and long-term maintenance. The best coatings for steel fabrications (offers an unlimited array of color potential and is especially good for handrails) are the new two-part polyurethane coatings, such as Dupont Imron. This type of coating far exceeds the life span of industrial enamels and stays glossy for seven to ten years.

Bottom right: New Orleans' stepped seawall of Works Progress Administration (WPA) vintage has provided excellent storm protection as well as continuous recreational access to Lake Pontchartrain *(top left)* along its five-mile entirety. *Bottom left:* The stepped gabion system offers the same solution for $600 per linear foot, instead of $2,500 per linear foot.

The most cost-effective material to use on any waterfront is pressure-treated wood. This material has been used on properties that are exposed directly to salt, which are now starting their third decade in perfect shape. Wood also provides warmth in a waterfront environment.

Roofing systems, surfaces, lighting, and walls all make up a broad range of design elements that can be used in conjunction with the materials used for stabilization to create a unified overall image that will effectively pack up the theme.

EFFECTIVE MANAGEMENT

Whether the waterfront development is to be public or private, long-range management will be crucial to its success. The facility must be aggressively managed to provide an excellent environment and services for the user. More and more public facilities (restricted by the Civil Service in terms of hiring, position definition, and reward criteria) are being managed by private nonprofit or tax-exempt organizations. The Municipal Yacht Harbor Management Corporation, in New Orleans, is an example of such a group. The harbor facility, with few landside facilities, but

Top right: Under the Aga Khan's effective management and his Consorzio Costa Smeralda, an entire community was taken from the conceptual stage to reality in less than ten years. Effective marketing and support systems, such as his creation of the airline Alisarda, made access desirable and easy.

Bottom right: Effective event programming of the waterfront means revenue and high usage. The Halter 200 offshore race brings 200,000 visitors to the stepped seawall of Lake Pontchartrain in New Orleans. The economic impact exceeded $4 million.

670 slips and 100 hundred boathouses charging market rates, nets well over $700,000 per year. When this waterfront was poorly managed ten years ago, it operated at a loss and had to be subsidized. Proper management, whether through a special development corporation, commission, or agency is crucial from the conceptual stage to the daily details of keeping the walkways clean and handrails painted. The management plan should include everyone who will be involved for overall coordination with the Port Authority, economic development foundations, parks departments, departments of trans-

portation, and so on. If coordination is not achieved, the development's progress will be slowed down and its long-term viability threatened. As contemporary society makes greater amounts of leisure time available, each recreational facility must compete more vigorously for its share of the market. Thus we are entering an era in which all major recreational facilities will be involved with the ''business of recreation,'' with their success or failure based on their capability for at least self-sufficiency. Organization and planning and advertising are essential, as is the need to continually promote the waterfront devel-

opment and to conceive of new events, activities, and reasons to return to the water's edge.

Return visitorship is the key ingredient to a waterfront's long-term success. If users make repeated visits; the facility will become a tradition, and, as such, its history and its impact on the city will be complete.

Bottom left: Gasparilla Day Festival in Tampa, with the main pirate ship about to seize the city of Tampa. *Bottom right:* A day-long event, the revenue exceeds $6 million and is one of the major yearly cultural events.

TAMPA TRIBUNE—BAYSHORE AERIAL PHOTOS/PHOTO LAB

BEGINNING THE PROJECT

The first step in any waterfront project is to develop an accurate base from which future plans can be made. This process need not be exorbitant. The individuals or group responsible for establishing this will need current information. It is amazing how often a developer will be given a ten-year-old survey base and be asked to develop long range plans for a dynamic new waterfront! Photogrammetric survey bases provide up-to-date aerial photographs and anywhere from .5- to 2-foot contours (vertical increment). The cost, for the five linear miles of Biloxi, Mississippi's waterfront, for instance, was under $15,000. The 5-mile photogrammetric survey for Bayshore Boulevard in Tampa, Florida cost less than $20,000 and included subsurface utility research and drafted bases at 200 and 50 scale. For a small waterfront park of 20 to 30 acres, the price might be as little as $2,000. The cost of a field survey would be astronomical and, without a fresh aerial photograph, contain errors difficult to trace and verify.

The next step should be a trip to the municipal, state, and regional archives, to the public library, or to those elderly individuals with the greatest local knowledge and the most photographs and even lithographs. Establishing a theme that will move people and meet their expectations of what the waterfront should be, or recapture what it was, will lead to its new

Top and *bottom right:* The Biloxi, Mississippi waterfront attempted to weave recreation into the prevalent inaccessible industrial edge. To mitigate objection from the fishermen, the open-planning process provided a basis for everyone to talk as neighbors, rather than as special-interest groups and adversaries.

image. The authenticity of that image will be based on historic documentation and the success or failure of the project to respond to the community's concerns. The City of Pascagoula, Mississippi is a center for the fishing industry and for ship building and is surrounded by barrier islands, a gulf, and an estuary. Yet, prior to recent waterfront development, there was no place to walk, sit, or eat at the water's edge, although historically an accessible area had existed before its demolition by hurricane. Research was conducted on the scale, details, image, and architecture of the old waterfront.

Armed with photographs, drawings, and current survey base maps, the potential developer must attempt to coordinate and form a concensus among all agencies requiring approval on issues such as circulation, access, transportation, land use, zoning, and environmental issues. Possible contiguous facilities, their enterprise zone potentials or special funding options should be reviewed. Financial reviews of other facilities and demographic data can often be assembled economically by working with the local Chamber of Commerce. By integrating all data, the initial theme and image of the project can take shape. How big will it be? How big *can* it be? What are the critical edges, and elements dependent on each other within? What if a portion of the project cannot be developed immediately—how will that affect the rest? All of these questions must be answered and a direction given that will yield a comprehensive, balanced, and self-contained project that will not only survive public scrutiny but also fire popular imagination.

Developing a Consensus
Perhaps forming a consensus can be described best as "taking your licks" in public long enough so that adversaries are eventually worn down by the merits of the potential waterfront development. The best way to achieve this successfully is through the open public process. By holding a series of forums, the public is led through the initial concept and subsequent detail design stages, as they listen, offer input, fight over issues, and formulate the basis of what their waterfront should be. The process allows for participation and the opportunity for the community to buy into the plan. This will provide short- and long-term benefits from greater ease in obtaining permits to attracting better tenants for the facilities operations. A good rule of thumb for these forums is one per month until the plan is resolved, followed by one large advertised public presentation with as much press coverage as possible. Fanfare at the completion of this planning effort should not be overlooked and, in fact, should serve to excite the community as the new beginning of the waterfront's development.

Organizing Management
To allow the project to move quickly, it is necessary for the developer and his or her management committee to gain political support, which is never accomplished without representation. The initial management committee might include representatives from the municipality or regional authority, the agencies that will be directly or indirectly affected, and those with specific expertise, such as sailors with knowledge of marinas and their needs, historians with an understanding of the property's legacy, and businesspeople who can package the development's land uses effectively. The waterfront must be their major priority, and they must be willing to fight, if necessary, to allow its needs to be met.

Left: The open-planning process allows for all issues to be aired, sometimes in a boisterous setting: It does, nonetheless, open the issues to discussion, which is essential for ultimate resolution and agreement.

In selecting the specific members of the committee it is important to be sure that those selected will attend all meetings and forums, and produce whatever follow-up is necessary. Many times prestigious committee members are chosen for their community prowess but are not effective because they are never there when needed. It is recommended that a private non-profit or tax-exempt set-up for project management be used. Such an organization will ultimately offer more flexibility, move more quickly, and operate more aggressively as a business. This will mean greater success to the waterfront development, while making all involved look good. Avoid, if at all possible, cumbersome public commissions restricted by Civil Service requirements, political appointments, and management by too many hands. The first priority is the waterfront development, and management should be the vehicle to bring it to realization within the most effective means possible.

Maintaining Momentum

During the course of the waterfront's development, together with the planning forums and promotional efforts, programming informational and media events will be necessary. Even if no dirt has been moved, staging events on the future site, or arranging other kinds of activities that will encourage the community's awareness of the waterfront are crucial.

Right: A typical organizational chart should delineate tasks, program, concepts, meeting and coordination dates, and costs. The entire effort is, in effect, mapped out at the beginning, allowing for everyone involved to maximize participation in the process.

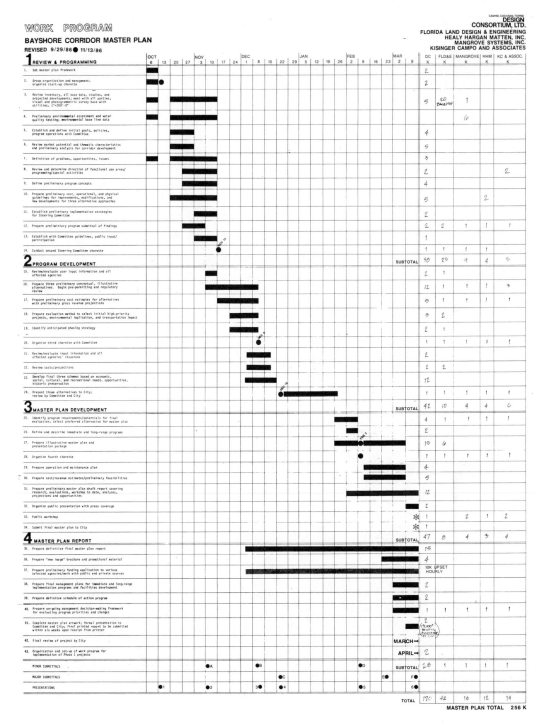

Whether it is through a fish fry, boat parade or race, concert or fair, the community should be made aware of the project's specific progress every four to six months. In Pascagoula, a city of 30,000 people, 10,000 inhabitants turned out recently for their first Blessing of the Fleet Festival. The desire to go down to the water's edge is powerful. Developers should use this power both to move the project forward and to maintain its momentum until opening day. Creating anticipation is, in essence, creating the market base that will be necessary for the project's fiscal success. Remembering that the leverage ratio is four to seven times the initial capital injection for the waterfront, financial success is important to both the development and its environs.

Planning the Opening Celebration
There is nothing like a spectacular party to stir a community and create support for a waterfront development. Jacksonville, Florida opened the 1.1-mile-long Southbank Riverwalk with the "world's longest chorus line," jugglers, mimes, musicians, dancers, food, fireworks and laser shows. The event spanned three days and left the community with the feeling that Jacksonville was beginning a new chapter in its history. A city that had grown from the river was reunited. From this initial opening, the riverwalk built up a weekend attendance of 7,000 visitors per day, in contrast to only two years ago when no one ventured to the waterfront.

Top left: Jacksonville's Southbank Riverwalk is now host to more than 7,000 people per average weekend, with up to 50,000 on holidays and event weekends *(bottom left).* Special events such as high diving off San Francisco's Pier 39 draw thousands of visitors annually.

Celebrations are important because they illustrate commitment to the development. They should be impressive but at the same time personal in feeling. The developer should seek out professional help in staging the opening, as the feeling and imagery provided by this event will launch the waterfront development. It is appropriate and advisable to utilize local foods, crafts, water activities, and music whenever possible. Interpretive and historical experiences should be provided in the process. And since this is the beginning of the development's operation, all activities should reiterate the essence of the project —its theme, image, and authenticity.

Bottom left: The opening day must be staged as the event of the year and, of course, culminate with an evening showing of pyrotechnics and laser beams *(right).*

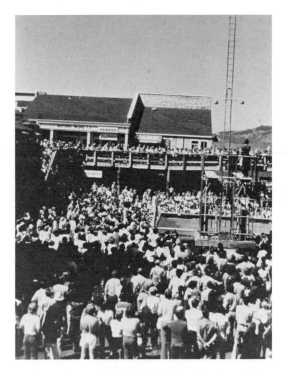

RECENT WATERFRONT DEVELOPMENTS

As the momentum for waterfront redevelopment continues to grow across the nation, the breadth of scale and the intensity are expanding proportionately. Cities containing from 10,000 to 10,000,000 people are attempting to transform their major resource into their major recreational facility. Some of the classic examples of the waterfront renascence of the last decade such as Boston, Baltimore, and New York have been joined by a diverse range of new developments. The following sampling represents a variety of recent waterfront projects, from seaside to riverside, from a grand city scale to small new communities. In all of those cases, access to the waterfront is the goal; development of activities and the creation or re-creation of a network of cultural facilities serving the community at the water's edge is the concept and theme.

NEW ORLEANS WATERFRONT

As the belle of the Mississippi, New Orleans has a rich waterfront legacy. But the Mississippi is only half of that legacy. Historically, Lake Pontchartrain and the Gulf of Mexico provided trade routes along which French, Spanish, and American traders would travel, bringing a rich mixture of cultures and a love for life at the water's edge. Originally an island on high ground founded by Iberville in 1719, the city expanded its edge to the shores of Lake Pontchartrain using Bayou Saint John, the old Basin, as the trade route. In the 1920s, the New Basin Canal was dug at the expense of thousands of Irish workers' lives to provide a new, larger waterway directly into the city's core. Majestic schooners with cargoes of lumber and various goods made their way through these waters to the transportation center in town, linking to the Mississippi River and the nation.

Waterfront areas such as West End, with its broad wooden decks, Spanish Fort, and Milneburg, a waterfront village out over the mud flats of Lake Pontchartrain, which was a stop for musicians on their way from the Storyville Whorehouse of Basin Street to the clubs on Bourbon Street, formed the basis for New Orleans

Top left: Biloxi, Mississippi's seafood industry docks serve as typical "before" situations.

Bottom left: Fort Lauderdale's indoor/outdoor rapport with the Intracoastal Waterway sets the example for a successful solution.

Facing page: Early line drawing by Nathanial Curtis, Sr., depicts New Orleans as a waterfront city surrounded by lake, river, and numerous canals for commercial and recreational use, all of which were lost to modernization.

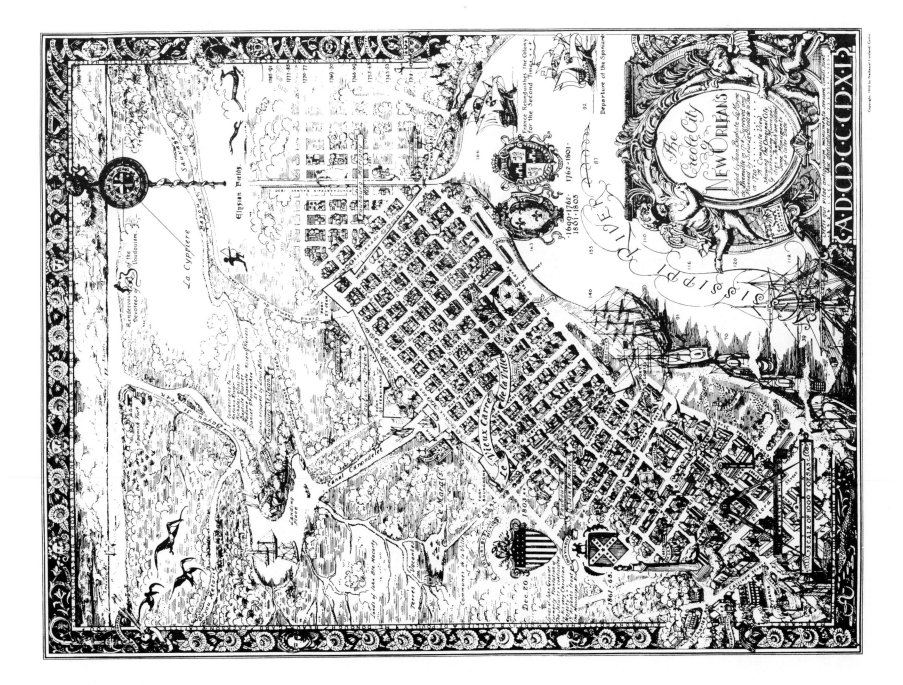

cultural motto "Le Bon Ton Roule". The scene was a romantic city, reminiscent of Amsterdam. Its working waterfront was lined with bars, restaurants, and working and pleasure craft, all side by side and exemplifying multiple-use at its best. But only thirty years after the New Basin Canal was dug in about 1900, it was filled in to provide an easy right-of-way for man's newest appendage, the automobile, along with the inevitable expressway. The Amsterdam of the United States was effectively killed without any real realization of what was being lost. What the automobile did not destroy, the government did.

Milneburg was destroyed because of codes, regulations, insurance issues, and for basically housing undesirables. It was replaced by Pontchartrain Beach, an amusement park that continued to operate until the early 1980s. At the same time as Pontchartrain Beach began, on the Mississippi River, wharves were built in a contiguous fashion all along the river's edge, backed by rail spurs, probably an effective means of loading and off-loading cargo, but a pattern that completely segregated the community from the water.

It wasn't until the early 1970s that the far-sighted Mayor Moon Landrieu saw the importance of returning the riverfront to the people of New Orleans. The fortuitous crashing of a freighter into one of the wharves allowed Jackson Square, the heart of the Vieux Carré, to once again be open to the river. The city, now surrounded by 12-foot levees, was united with the edge by Washington Artillery Park, which led visitors over the floodwall via ramps and stairs to the Moonwalk, the first chance to sit at the water's edge. Stabilized by riprap, the project would have been far more aesthetic and usable to pedestrians if stepped gabions had been used to provide more access to the river. Renovations included the Old French Market, one of the first marketplaces in the United States, and recent additions to this complex are the renovation of the Jax Brewery, Canal Place Shopping Mall, and a new $40-million aquarium and riverfront

Top left: Roustabouts on the Mississippi Batture, circa 1885. Note wooden decking and embankments to which the paddlewheelers moored and *(bottom left)* the Moonwalk, a revisiting of river access some 70 years later.

park. These facilities will link the entire waterfront of the French Quarter to its sister city, the American Sector along the Mississippi River. Already developed is the 160,000 square-foot Rouse Riverwalk and a major new Convention Center, which, when expanded, will maintain 1 million square feet. This overall waterfront development will have taken nearly three decades to realize and will serve the primary industry to the city—tourism.

The redevelopment of the Lake Pontchartrain waterfront has been more difficult to achieve than New Orleans' return to the Mississippi River. The lakefront was stabilized by a Works Projects Administration-era seawall of stepped design. With a moderate wave-energy level (a fetch of 75 miles for Northwesters to build up steam), the stepped seawall has performed admirably over the last 50 years. Allowing for continuous access to the edge, it has served to promote activities such as fishing, swimming, and crabbing, rather than separate pedestrians from the water's edge, as many wave de-energizing seawalls do.

An adequate parkway and recreational facilities line the 5.5-mile lakefront, which is composed completely of landfill. It is a facility enjoyed by thousands, but the legacy of the New Orleans lakefront is supported only by the West End development of slipshod and poorly run seafood restaurants and bars with inadequate management and programming. One of the outstanding facilities is the Municipal Yacht Harbor, which, under public/private management exists on a self-sufficient basis and provides 670 slips, 130 boathouses, two yacht clubs and waterfront park to the city. It is hoped that at some point a substantial theme will be pursued to return West End to its former grandeur and to create a new waterfront development for New Orleans.

The Pontchartrain Beach Development represents an attempt to transform a defunct amusement park into an exciting new waterfront residential community. The development was proposed as five modular phases. The architecture was articulated so as to allow each module a view of Lake Ponchartrain, while providing specific amenities to each cluster. The units were stacked and stepped back, permitting multiple use of roof and balcony, much like at Positano, Italy. The overall "texture" of the development was a patchwork quilt of five different treatments, which could be woven together to respond to the individual owner's choices, yet giving the result a feeling of a true city facade.

The central core provided a 3-acre pool, shops, restaurants, a plaza, and rental facilities on a beach that was ecologically designed to respond to prevailing conditions. Although the final solution has nothing to do with the scale and texture of Milneburg, which was on the same site ninety years earlier, it serves as a functional response to the contemporary city's desire to live at the water's edge and takes into account the 18-foot-high storm protection walls that surround the below-sea-level city.

Project Criteria

Name: New Orleans Riverfront Park and Aquarium
Location: New Orleans, Louisiana
Date completed: 1991 (projected)
Size: 70,000 square feet; Aquarium, 20 acres total development,
Cost: $40 million

Description of Project Area Prior to Improvement
Underutilized wharves; part of the Mississippi River industrial complex, which essentially cut off all pedestrian access to the river's edge and blocked view from the historic Vieux Carré (French Quarter) to the river and its traffic.

Results of Project Completion
Jobs: 3,500 during construction; 350 permanent
Tax Base: $53.5 million per year
Events: Numerous waterfront events, including river festivals, concerts, and laser and fireworks displays
Tourism increase: 250,000 new tourists; 850,000 visitors projected
Characteristics: Access to and entertainment and recreation directly on the waterfront

Unique Attributes of the Project
Architecture and site: Riverfront wharf vernacular; Waterfront Park is a reiteration of the early New Orleans riverfront
Theme: Waterfront
Basis for theme: historic New Orleans, Riverfront Culture
Land use: Recreational surrounded by hotels, restaurants, festival marketplace, commerical, industrial port, and residential facilities

Project status
In process. Funding came through a major bond election, which achieved a 71 percent to 29 percent victory because of the tremendous orchestration and lobbying efforts by the Friends of the Audubon Zoo and Audubon Park Commission who will be the ultimate managers of the facility.

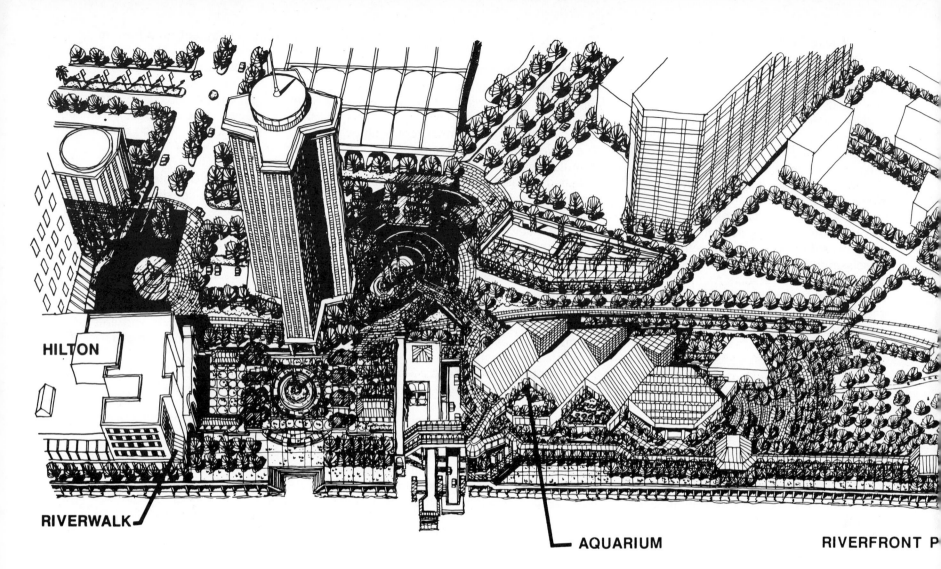

HILTON

RIVERWALK

AQUARIUM

RIVERFRONT P

The New Orleans Aquarium and Riverfront Park attempt to link the two historic villages, the French Quarter and the American Sector, into one continuous waterfront park, featuring a great lawn on the spot where the explorer Bienville first set claim to the city founding for France.

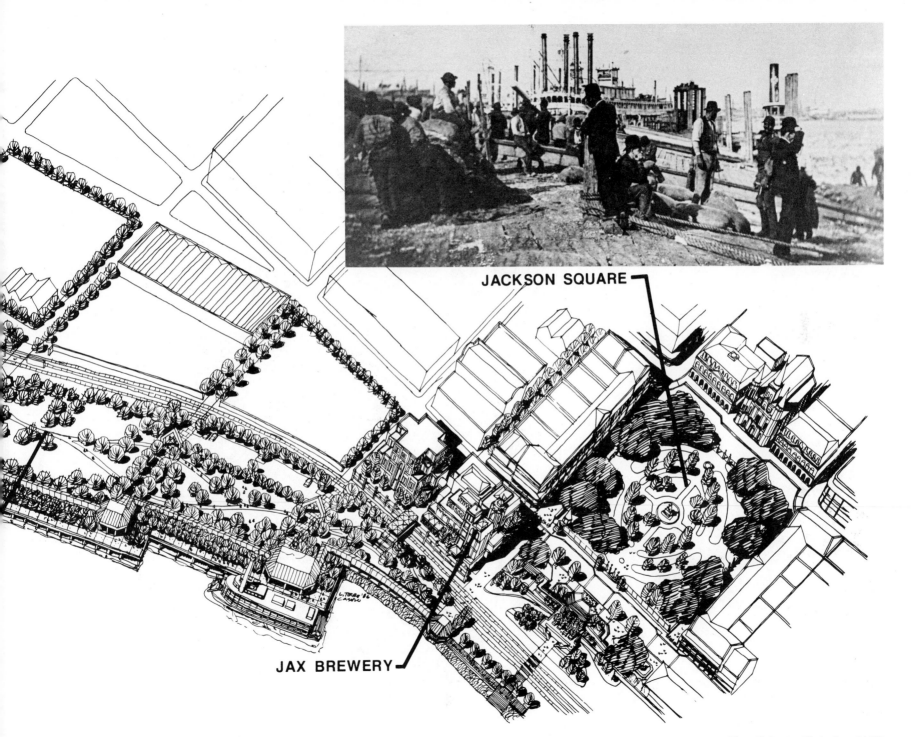

JACKSON SQUARE

JAX BREWERY

Top, center, and *bottom left:* The new river-front takes the place of the industrial edge of wharves, which have obstructed access to the edge for the last half century.

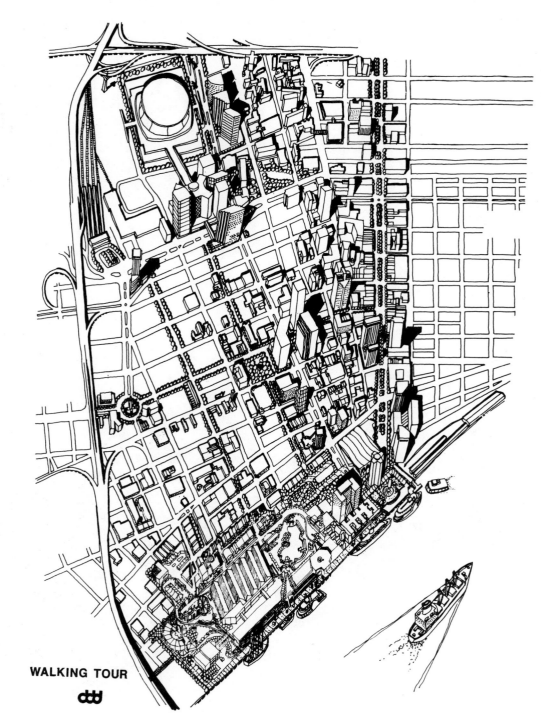

WALKING TOUR

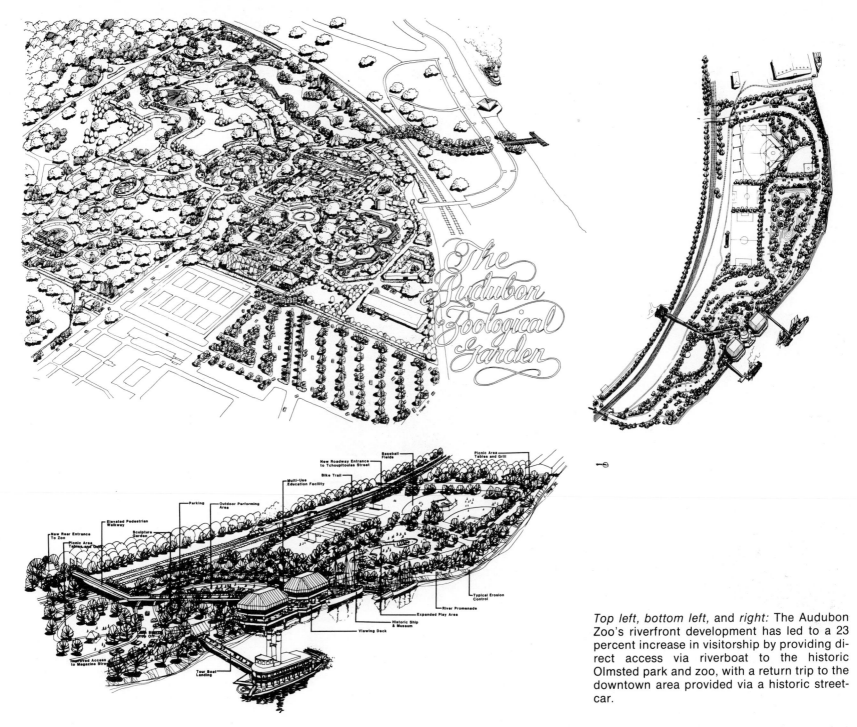

The Audubon Zoological Garden

Top left, bottom left, and *right:* The Audubon Zoo's riverfront development has led to a 23 percent increase in visitorship by providing direct access via riverboat to the historic Olmsted park and zoo, with a return trip to the downtown area provided via a historic streetcar.

New Rear Entrance To Zoo
Picnic Area Tables and Grill
Elevated Pedestrian Walkway
Sculpture Garden
Parking
Outdoor Performing Area
Multi-Use Education Facility
Bike Trail
New Roadway Entrance to Tchoupitoulas Street
Baseball Fields
Picnic Area Tables and Grill
Improved Access to Magazine Street
Tour Boat Landing
Viewing Deck
Historic Ship & Museum
Expanded Play Area
River Promenade
Typical Erosion Control

COURTESY THE HISTORIC NEW ORLEANS COLLECTION

Project Criteria

Name: Pontchartrain Beach Development
Location: New Orleans, Louisiana
Date Completed: project abandoned
size: 1 million square feet; 97 acres, regional population 1.2 million
Cost: $75 million

Description of Project Area Prior to Improvement

Formerly historic Milneburg village, later Pontchartrain Beach Amusement Park, which functioned until the mid 1980s. Bulkheads and beach were in place, with only remaining historic feature being the lighthouse.

Results of Project Completion

Jobs: 2,000
Tax base: $2 million per year, excluding sales tax on commercial areas
Events: boat races, rentals, holiday celebrations
Tourism increase: 100,000 per year
Characteristics: a major waterfront residential community directly on the lake in a city that prevents waterfront development by virtue of its 18-foot-high levees, which effectively cut off views and linkages to adjacent housing developments.

The historic waterfront developments of New Orleans lakefront were West End *(top and center left)* with the New Basin Canal, Spanish Fort *(bottom left)* and Milneburg.

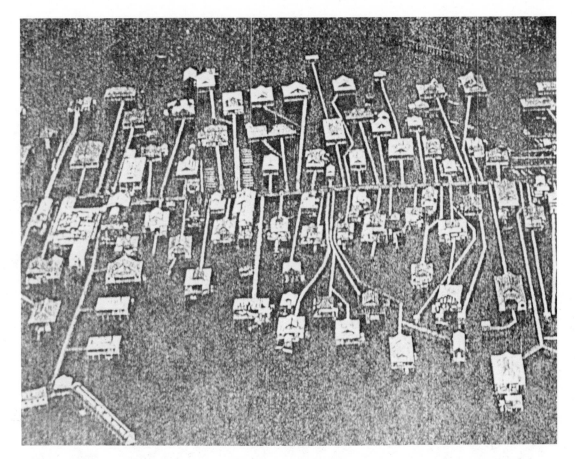

Top left: Schooners at head of New Basin Canal. June-16-1929.

The New Basin Canal, circa, 1929, delineates its European image and function, serving as a transportation conduit for commerce and recreation to West End pavilions and restraints on the lake *(center left)*.

The maze of boardwalks of Milneburg *(top right)* created a unique city. *Bottom right:* The community's intra-linkage was based on convenience and friendship.

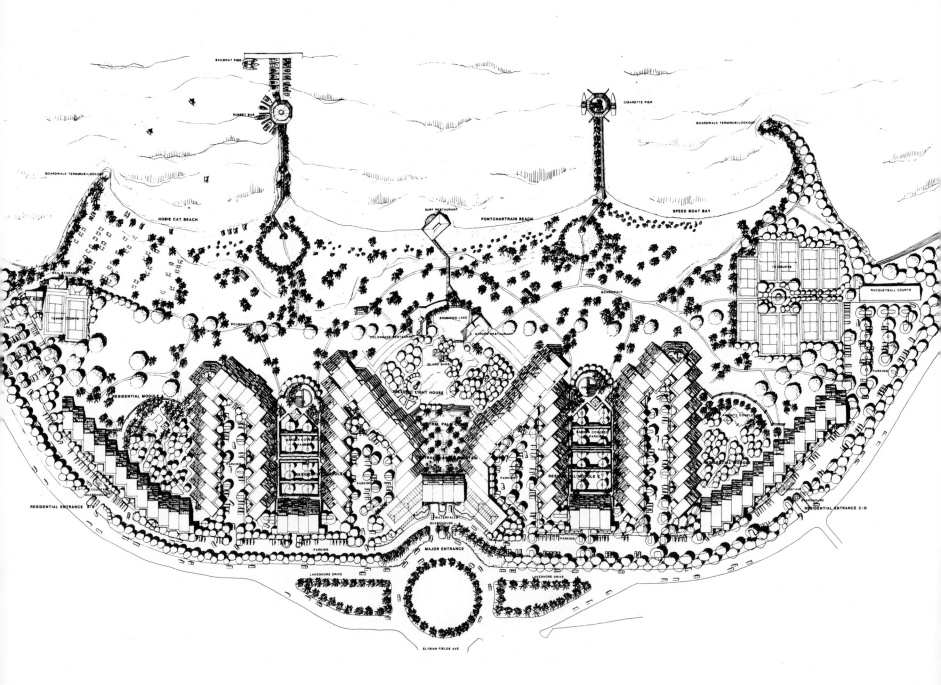

Unique Attributes of the Project

Architecture and site: Flat site, which was stepped vertically to multiple-level residential units

Theme: southern waterfront development with beach orientation

Basis for theme: layout of existing site and history of previously existing Milneburg

Land use: office, specialty, residential with ancillary commercial facilities, shops, and four restaurants

Project Status

The project failed as the developer attempted to develop another scheme that offered fewer than half of its units a lake view and was also costly—$200 per square foot in a local market that had never supported sales in excess of $100 per foot. Presently in reorganization.

ENTRY TREATMENT

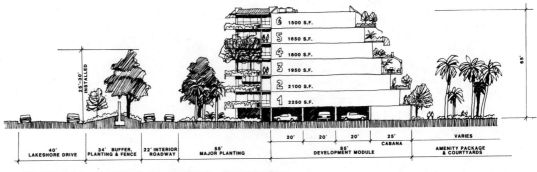

TYPICAL DEVELOPMENT SECTION

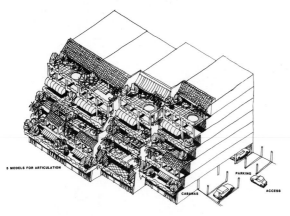

PONTCHARTRAIN BEACH DEVELOPMENT

Facing page, top right, center right, and *bottom left:* Pontchartrain Beach Development.

Bottom right: Pontchartrain Beach circa 1975, prior to being closed to the public in the early 1980s.

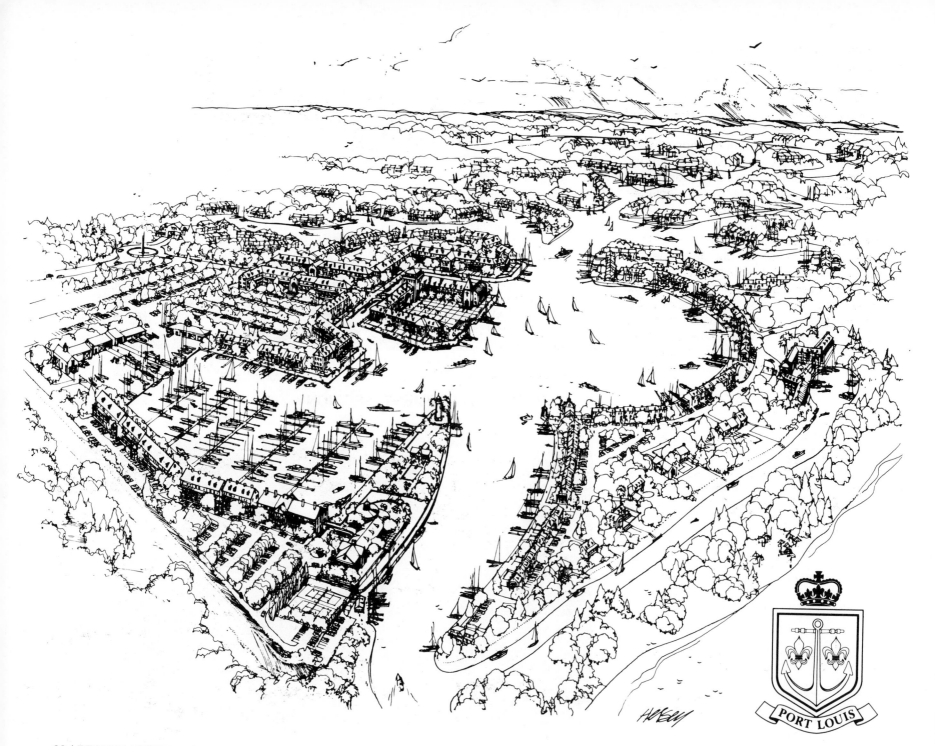

PORT LOUIS

PORT LOUIS SAILING VILLAGE

A new waterfront village was proposed and partially completed on the northern shore of Lake Pontchartrain. Modeled after Port Grimaud (see page 106.), Port Louis Sailing Village attempted to claim from the low-lying fields of southern Louisiana a romantic residential village with a water orientation and a commitment to boating. The ambitious facility provides a good example of the difficulty in translating a successful development concept from one area (France) to another (southern Louisiana). Not only was the translation in architectural style difficult (barrel tile and stucco to weatherboard and seal-tab roof), but the economic research did not prove in-depth enough to ascertain that the economy had never been sound, and with the oil industry taking a sudden plunge, financial capability was nonexistent at the critical marketing time. Although the project has merit and will perhaps be adopted by another developer or financial institution, success will also depend on regional population growth. At the time this development went on the market, several other projects with a closer proximity to New Orleans (where most people work) were also proposed. Unlike New York or California, the idea of a one-and-one-half-hour drive to work is one whose time has not yet come to the New Orleans area.

Port Louis serves as a critical example of a worthy concept whose base requirements were not analyzed and met. It underlines the importance of not being

Facing page: With a central basin having the city center plaza as a backdrop, the proposed school offered an exciting waterfront potential for Port Louis, Louisiana (*top* and *bottom right*).

overcome by the romance of a development without knowing what the market parameters really are.

Project Criteria
Name: Port Louis Sailing Village
Location: St. Tammany Parish, Louisiana
Date Completed: Phase I-A (53 units), February 1986
Size: Phase I, 109 acres
Cost: Phase I-A (20 acres), $7.5 million

Description of Project Area Prior to Improvement
Leveed and drained marshland on Lake Pontchartrain, previously used for farming. Land was approximately +1:0 MSL and cleared with the exception of a stand of scrub trees in a low-lying area of the site

Results of Project Completion
Jobs: during construction over 60 jobs were created and over $15 million from France invested in Louisiana
Tax base: $8 million in new housing
Events: not available
Tourism Increase: not available
Characteristics: isolated; relaxed during week; active and animated on weekends

Unique Attributes of the Project
Architecture and site: rural Louisiana vernacular; direct access to open water and deep water mooring for sailboats.

Top and *bottom left:* Some of the initial weaknesses in the project appear in the adaptation of the Louisiana cottage to a Mediterranean zero-lot style. What works well in barrel tile and stucco did not quite succeed in clapboard and seal-tab roof.

Theme: Every home on the water and fee-simple ownership creates illusion of permanency through eclectic architectural detailing

Basis for theme: master plan inspired by Port Grimaud, France

Land use: Phase I-A was to include commercial, residential, office, and specialty space to be built over a ten-year period.

Project Status

Project currently stopped because of lack of continued sales and additional financing.

Top right: The concept was excellent, a return to the romantic lakeside of West End. The construction site before *(bottom left)* and after *(bottom right)* the basin was opened.

BILOXI, MISSISSIPPI

A unique and historic port village dating back to the 1700s, Biloxi succumbed, like many other cities, to industrialization of its waterfront. The 1983 master plan, spearheaded by Mayor Gerald Blessy, sought to reunite the community with the water's edge, by establishing a successful balance between recreation and the seafood industry.

Out of the many sites studied in the

plan, the Point Cadet area was designated for first-phase development. This involved reestablishing the old fishing village area while providing much-needed marina slips, a festival marketplace, a water park, hotels, and numerous recreational amenities adjacent to the existing 500,000-gallon aquarium, which had been built earlier under state funds. Land acquisition was handled by Housing and Urban Development's Community Block Development 108 Program, under which a community can receive several years entitlement in advance if project development is termed acceptable. A consensus was achieved through year-long public meetings for this 45-acre site as well as for several other new facilities, including a beach nourishment and management program, fishing piers, and a 500-slip commercial marina, which provided its own environmental mitigation by the shaving down of adjacent uplands and by creating a themed wetland park. Additional mitigation for other parts of the development was accomplished by the public acquisition and

establishment of protection for the adjacent barrier island, which was under pressure for commercial development. The eventual solution will provide for a successful relationship with adjacent fishing harbors and seafood packaging plants, allowing visitors and residents to visit and enjoy these working areas while being linked to a complex fabric of recreational amenities. The project revitalized both the physical and psychological well-being of the community through the successful rebirth of Biloxi's waterfront heritage.

Project Criteria
Name: Biloxi Waterfront
Location: Biloxi, Mississippi
Date Completed: In process
Size: Festival marketplace, 50,000 square feet; 160-room hotel; waterpark; 400-slip marina; Regional population 300,000; city population 30,000
Cost: Phase I, $22 million, Phase II, $18 million

Description of Project Area Prior to Improvement
Basically industrial waterfront edge, dedicated to fishing industry; obstructed pedestrian access to the waterfront; extreme shortage of commercial and pleasure craft slips; historic water-oriented character of city diminished except for man-made beach areas.

Top left: A regatta in front of the old Biloxi Yacht Club, which later succumbed to a hurricane. The present club is in a brick veneer structure on concrete slab, an unfortunate decision.

Bottom left: Life at the water's edge, circa 1920. The barrier island, Deer Island, is in the background.

Results of Project Completion

Jobs: 1,400 new or retained jobs

Tax base: $1.5 million in new tax base; $18 million in gross sales

Events: Blessing of the Fleet, Christmas Boat Parade, Point Cadet Festival, holiday events

Tourism increase: 1 million new visitors

Characteristics: a major enhancement of a historic waterfront that will successfully coexist with industry.

Unique Attributes of the Project

Architecture and site: gulf coast theme emphasizing proper scale and orientation to facilities in accordance with weather cycles.

Theme: gulf coast fishing village

Basis for theme: Biloxi is and has been historically one of the seafood industry leaders on the Gulf of Mexico

Land use: commercial, industrial, residential, office, recreational, aquarium, and festival marketplace

Project Status

After establishing a public consensus through an open-planning process and some twelve public forums over the course of one year, effective management through the creation of the public/private Point Cadet Development Corporation has successfully brought the initial phases to fruition.

Top right: The seafood industry was the inspiration for special design and function and literally the subbase of the city's waterfront lands, composed of oyster shells.

Bottom right: Bob Landry's poster depicts the design of vessels of the Mississippi Sound.

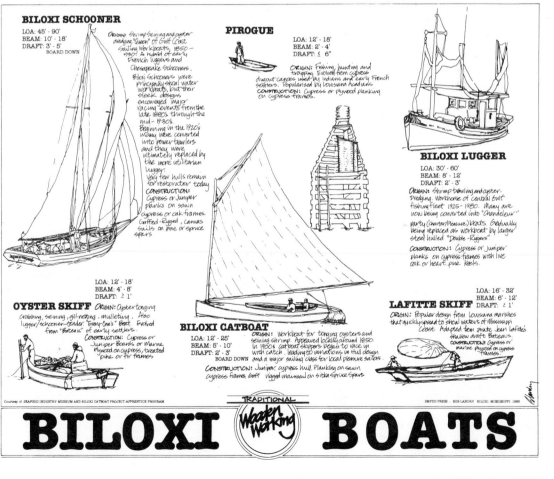

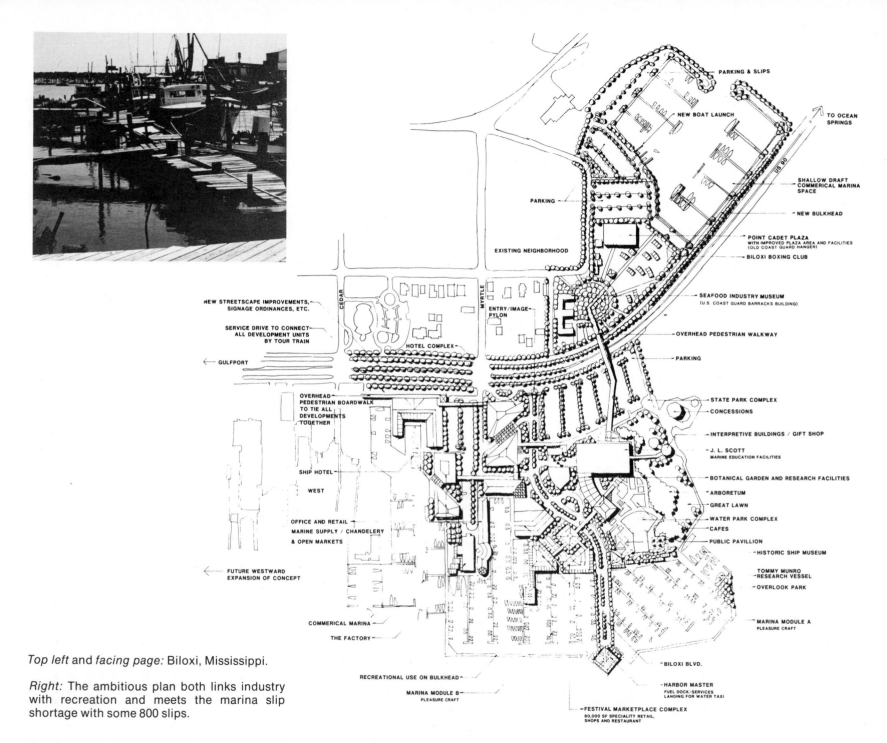

PARKING & SLIPS

NEW BOAT LAUNCH

TO OCEAN
SPRINGS

US 90

SHALLOW DRAFT
COMMERICAL MARINA
SPACE

PARKING

NEW BULKHEAD

POINT CADET PLAZA
WITH IMPROVED PLAZA AREA AND FACILITIES
(OLD COAST GUARD HANGER)

EXISTING NEIGHBORHOOD

BILOXI BOXING CLUB

NEW STREETSCAPE IMPROVEMENTS,
SIGNAGE ORDINANCES, ETC.

CEDAR

MYRTLE

ENTRY/IMAGE
PYLON

SEAFOOD INDUSTRY MUSEUM
(U.S. COAST GUARD BARRACKS BUILDING)

SERVICE DRIVE TO CONNECT
ALL DEVELOPMENT UNITS
BY TOUR TRAIN

HOTEL COMPLEX

OVERHEAD PEDESTRIAN WALKWAY

← GULFPORT

PARKING

OVERHEAD
PEDESTRIAN BOARDWALK
TO TIE ALL
DEVELOPMENTS
TOGETHER

STATE PARK COMPLEX

CONCESSIONS

INTERPRETIVE BUILDINGS / GIFT SHOP

SHIP HOTEL

J. L. SCOTT
MARINE EDUCATION FACILITIES

WEST

BOTANICAL GARDEN AND RESEARCH FACILITIES

ARBORETUM

GREAT LAWN

OFFICE AND RETAIL

WATER PARK COMPLEX

MARINE SUPPLY / CHANDELERY
& OPEN MARKETS

CAFES

PUBLIC PAVILLION

HISTORIC SHIP MUSEUM

← FUTURE WESTWARD
EXPANSION OF CONCEPT

TOMMY MUNRO
RESEARCH VESSEL

OVERLOOK PARK

MARINA MODULE A
PLEASURE CRAFT

COMMERICAL MARINA

THE FACTORY

BILOXI BLVD.

RECREATIONAL USE ON BULKHEAD

HARBOR MASTER
FUEL DOCK/SERVICES
LANDING FOR WATER TAXI

MARINA MODULE B
PLEASURE CRAFT

FESTIVAL MARKETPLACE COMPLEX
80,000 SF SPECIALITY RETAIL,
SHOPS AND RESTAURANT

Top left and *facing page:* Biloxi, Mississippi.

Right: The ambitious plan both links industry
with recreation and meets the marina slip
shortage with some 800 slips.

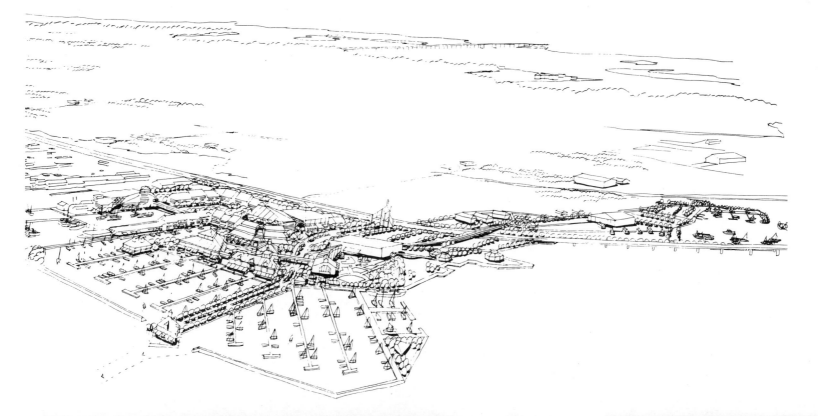

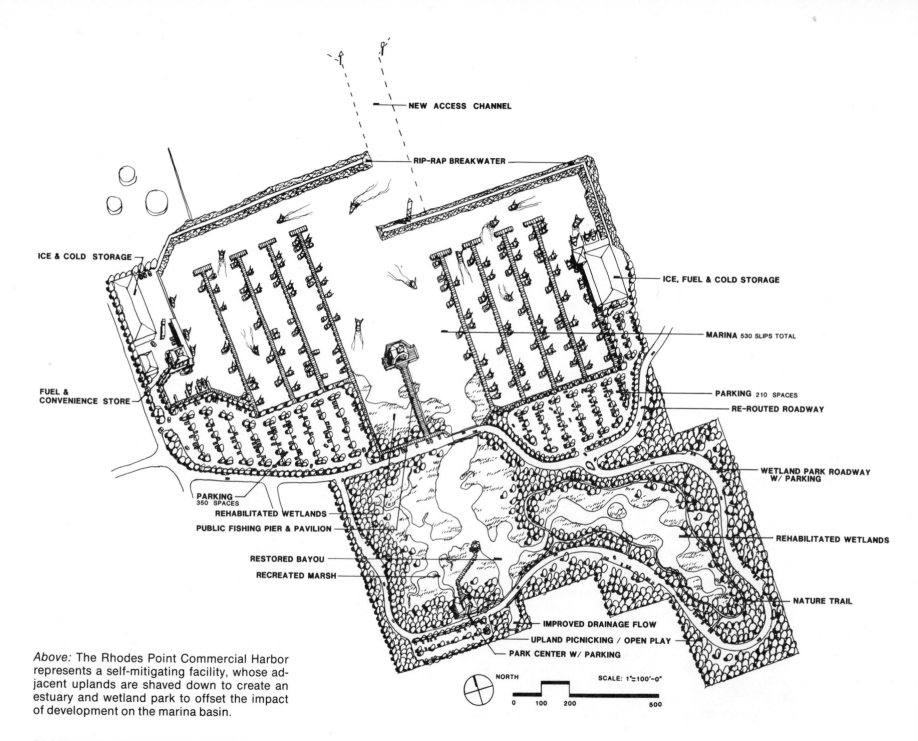

NEW ACCESS CHANNEL

RIP-RAP BREAKWATER

ICE & COLD STORAGE

ICE, FUEL & COLD STORAGE

MARINA 530 SLIPS TOTAL

FUEL & CONVENIENCE STORE

PARKING 210 SPACES

RE-ROUTED ROADWAY

WETLAND PARK ROADWAY W/ PARKING

PARKING 350 SPACES

REHABILITATED WETLANDS

PUBLIC FISHING PIER & PAVILION

REHABILITATED WETLANDS

RESTORED BAYOU

RECREATED MARSH

NATURE TRAIL

IMPROVED DRAINAGE FLOW

UPLAND PICNICKING / OPEN PLAY

PARK CENTER W/ PARKING

NORTH

SCALE: 1"≃100'-0"

0   100   200   500

Above: The Rhodes Point Commercial Harbor represents a self-mitigating facility, whose adjacent uplands are shaved down to create an estuary and wetland park to offset the impact of development on the marina basin.

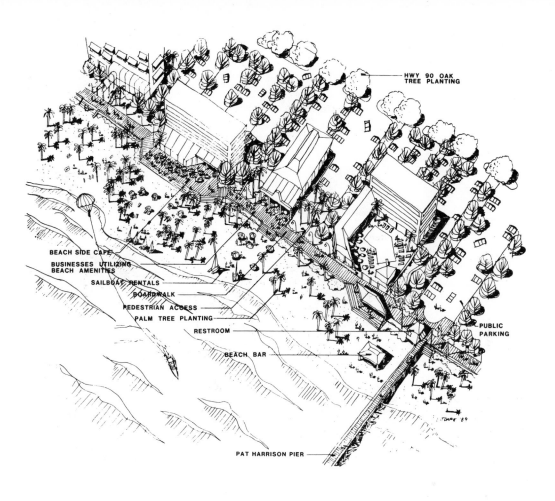

HWY 90 OAK TREE PLANTING

BEACH SIDE CAFE
BUSINESSES UTILIZING BEACH AMENITIES
SAILBOAT RENTALS
BOARDWALK
PEDESTRIAN ACCESS
PALM TREE PLANTING
RESTROOM
BEACH BAR
PUBLIC PARKING

PAT HARRISON PIER

Above: The overall plan's success starts with community image after the urban corridors. Landscaping, sign, and zoning ordinances seek to create a new, higher-quality image.

Below: All businesses were redirected to use their frontage on the sand beaches rather than turn their backs to it. As simple as this concept seems, it went without support for decades.

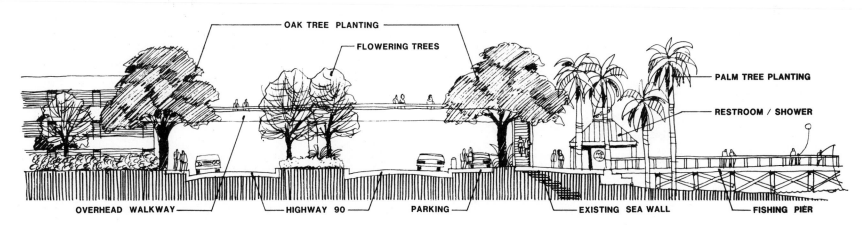

OAK TREE PLANTING
FLOWERING TREES
PALM TREE PLANTING
RESTROOM / SHOWER

OVERHEAD WALKWAY — HIGHWAY 90 — PARKING — EXISTING SEA WALL — FISHING PIER

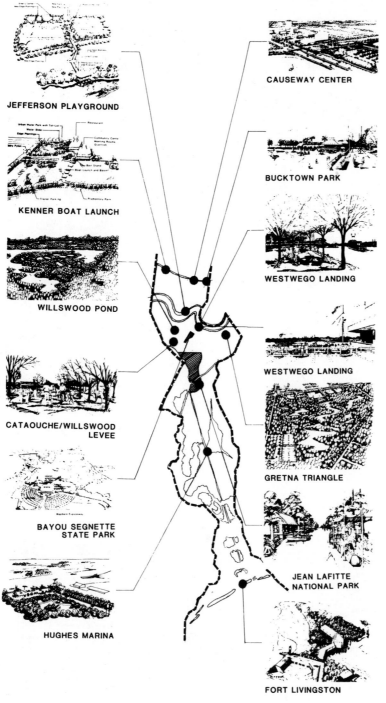

JEFFERSON PLAYGROUND

KENNER BOAT LAUNCH

WILLSWOOD POND

CATAOUCHE/WILLSWOOD LEVEE

BAYOU SEGNETTE STATE PARK

HUGHES MARINA

CAUSEWAY CENTER

BUCKTOWN PARK

WESTWEGO LANDING

WESTWEGO LANDING

GRETNA TRIANGLE

JEAN LAFITTE NATIONAL PARK

FORT LIVINGSTON

Left: The proposed master plan attempts to connect and overlap the different zones of the Parish with proposed recreational use throughout the Parish. The first zone is the Lake Pontchartrain Linear Park, which would include the Bucktown Park, Causeway Center, Bonnabel Boat Launch, and Kenner Boat Launch developments. Next would be the levee systems on both banks of the Mississippi River, including the Jefferson Playground/ Overlook, and the Westwego Landing developments. The swamp/ marshland condition which comprises the majority of the Parish could include such projects as the Willswood Pond area, the Cataouche/Willswood Levee areas, and the use of the Bayou Segnette State Park and Jean Lafitte National Park. The last zone and the southernmost point of the Parish would be the barrier islands, where a development utilizing Fort Livingston would round out a Parish-wide recreational system. This system, for the first time, will be instrumental in creating a united Jefferson Parish.

JEFFERSON PARISH RECREATION MASTER PLAN

A major urban community of 600,000 people, Jefferson Parish, Louisiana covers 2,000 square miles, much of which is surrounded or bisected by Lake Pontchartrain, the Mississippi River, and the Gulf of Mexico. Without a budget capable of developing new recreational facilities, and already operating existing facilities at a deficit, the municipality found itself short some 2,000 acres of needed recreation facilities. The ensuing master plan considered the lake, river, and gulf resources as potential revenue-providing recreational facilities, including the use of storm-protection levees for camping and cabin areas. With over twenty new proposed facilities, the parish could in a logically phased sequence pay for each one through revenue bonds and subsequent self-sufficient operation, thus allowing for the staging of future projects. Waterfront development would include boat rentals and charters, meeting facilities, commercial sub-lets, and vacation facilities as well as river taxis, arrangements for tours, and event complexes. An urban lakefront development would provide recreational use along with consolidation and creation of a new downtown waterfront city center. As delineated by initial pro forma, the entire $40 million system could be realized over a seven-year period, using various grants in the early years for organization, infrastructure, and set-up.

Major nodal developments propose a comprehensive overall system which would open up Lake Pontchartrain *(facing page, top right)* and the Mississippi River *(facing page, bottom right)* to active and passive recreational uses.

The public has responded positively to the concept of visitor fees at public park facilities to promote better security, maintenance, and quality of facility. What remains to be accomplished is the organization of an enterprise commission with the specific mandate and interest to pursue the business of recreation and realize the master plan.

Project Criteria
Name: Jefferson Parish Recreation Master Plan
Location: Jefferson Parish, Louisiana
Date completed: 1985
Size: Comprehensive recreation nodal development plan for 2,000 square miles of community; regional population 600,000
Cost: $40 million

Description of Project Area Prior to Improvement
As a sister community to New Orleans, with a comparable population of 600,000, the parish has inadequate recreational facilities and funds with which to build them. Bordered by Lake Pontchartrain, the Mississippi River, and the Gulf of Mexico, great waterfront potential existed, but there was little access or use other than by hunters and fishermen.

Results of Project Completion
Jobs: 350 to 400
Tax base: self-sufficient operation
Events: waterfront festivals, races, holiday events
Tourism increase: 200,000 per year
Characteristics: A community surrounded by water would gain access to its waterfront for the first time since the 1800s.

Unique Attributes of the Project
Architecture and site: southern Louisiana architecture woven into the many lakes, marshes, estuaries, and gulf coast sites
Theme: Southern Louisiana village
Basis for theme: Historic precedent
Land use: Passive and active recreational facilities

Project Status
Awaiting funding by municipality. The problem with the business of recreation by pro forma to municipalities is that they are basically not business-oriented and thus find it difficult to approach on a revenue-bond basis. Growing public sentiment in favor of paying for high-quality and secure recreational facilities is changing the historic bureaucratic approach, and it is hoped that this will give impetus toward starting the entire development program.

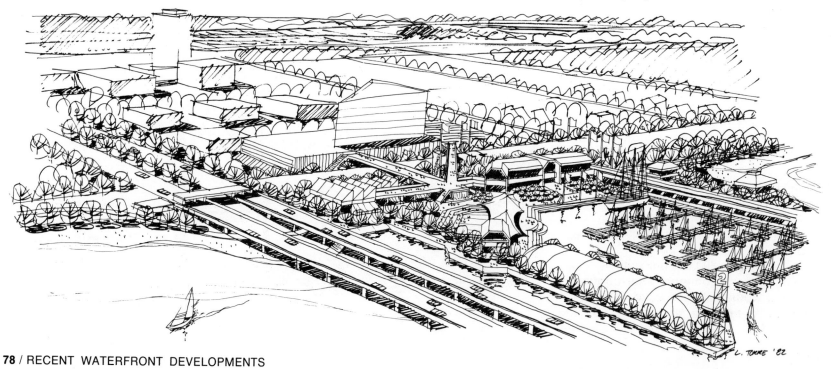

A vibrant new downtown waterfront would make the first real linkage of Jefferson Parish to its waterfront. Camping cabins along the parish's perimeter to the marshlands would be lined with overnight rental cabins with a five-minute river linkage to urban New Orleans. Bayou towns would connect all the way south to the barrier islands.

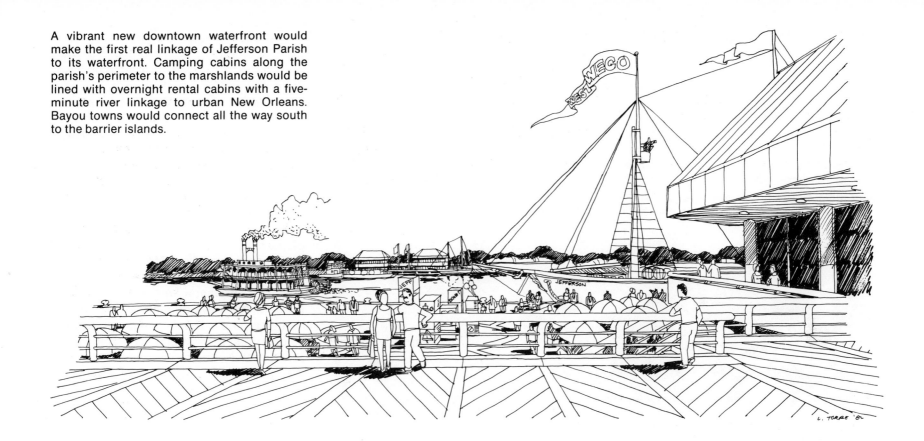

MISSISSIPPI SAND BEACHES

Of the approximate 100 miles of frontage on the Gulf of Mexico, the State of Mississippi maintains some 31 linear miles of man-made sand beach. The beach was pumped in to protect a stepped seawall whose section design was similar to that of New Orleans—but with a fetch of over 600 miles of open gulf waters and located in a hurricane impact zone, it had been severely damaged. The irony of this pragmatic solution was that this protective pillow of sand, used to protect the seawall, became the active economic basis of the cities of southern Mississippi as beach use necessitated hotels, condominiums, restaurants, and a myriad of recreational facilities. The drawback was that every ten years the beach eroded away from 300 feet in width to 200 feet or essentially 50 percent of its total volume because of wind and water.

The 1986 master plan provided for a more ecologically oriented beach section, planted with grasses, dunes, pines, and oak—essentially a replication of the adjacent barrier islands. With the 20 percent added volume of pumped sand needed for creating the dunes, the beach's projected longevity went from ten to forty years, providing crucial economic impact. Visual enhancement was a second benefit of the plan. Previously the beach had been flat and barren, with no shaded areas.

Another positive result was the location of parking facilities between the seawall and dune line, allowing for adequate parking below the sight of the roadway. By establishing pay-parking, the passive sections of the development would be self-sufficient. With more intensive nodal developments, recreational facilities, restaurants, rentals, and other related waterfront facilities would provide a positive financial management picture for the entire six-city, 31-mile corridor development. To ensure proper management and high-level maintenance of the development, a special waterfront commission, designed to analyze the economic and ecological importance of the beaches, was appointed, with representation from each city and county.

Project Criteria
Name: Mississippi Sand Beaches
Location: southern Mississippi gulf coast
Date completed: 1986
Size: 31 linear miles; regional population 300,000
Cost: $30 million

Left: Stretching 31 miles in length, the man-made sand beaches serve as the number one economic resource in the southern half of the state.

Description of Project Area Prior to Improvement

Pumped-in sand beach in front of stepped seawall damaged by hurricane storm waters; underutilized and environmentally unstable.

Results of Project Completion

Jobs: 2,000 to 3,000

Tax base: self-sufficient

Events: beach activities, boat races, holidays, fleet blessings, waterfront festivals, recreational activities

Tourism increase: 200,000 to 300,000 tourists

Characteristics: A more aesthetic and environmentally stable shore area

Unique Attributes of the Project

Architecture and site: southern Mississippi vernacular, Gulf Coast Barrier Island development section

Theme: same

Basis of theme: logical iteration of the community and environment

Land use: commercial, office, specialty, residential, industrial

Project Status

The sand beach is presently being pumped in and the waterfront commission has been formed. It is instructive to note that the effort was successfully accomplished in one year of public meetings and development of a consenus of support.

Right: The instability of Sand Beach, Mississippi's beach, is based on the simplicity of section design. With the addition of dunes, grasses, pines and oaks, the ecological section replicates the complexity and stability of the barrier islands.

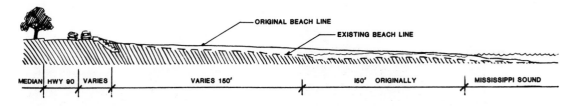

EXISTING BEACH SECTION

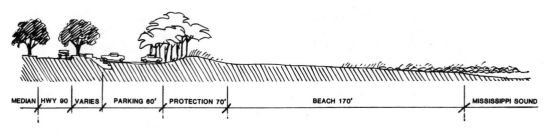

PROPOSED BEACH SECTION
CATEGORY 1

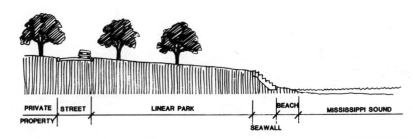

EXISTING BEACH SECTION
NORTH BAY ST. LOUIS

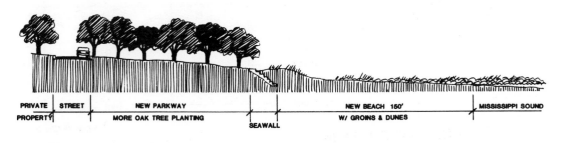

PROPOSED BEACH SECTION
NORTH BAY ST. LOUIS

TYPICAL HWY 90 VIEW
CATEGORY III

ELEVATION
TYPICAL RESTROOM / SHOWER
IN STREET RIGHT OF WAY

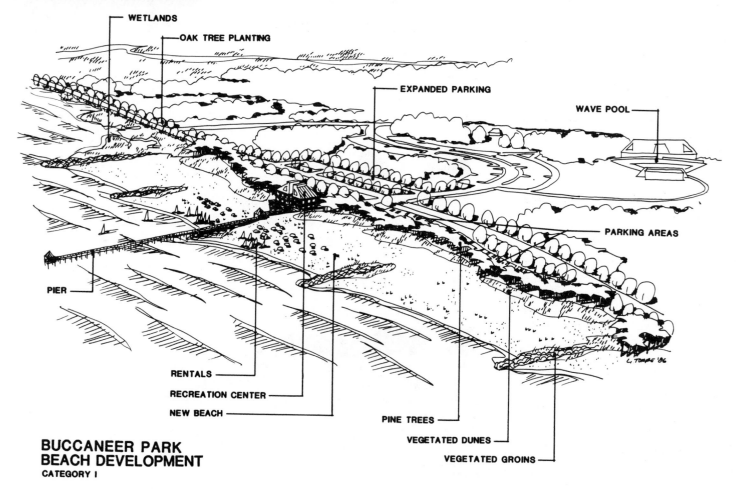

WETLANDS

OAK TREE PLANTING

EXPANDED PARKING

WAVE POOL

PARKING AREAS

PIER

RENTALS

RECREATION CENTER

NEW BEACH

PINE TREES

VEGETATED DUNES

VEGETATED GROINS

**BUCCANEER PARK
BEACH DEVELOPMENT**
CATEGORY I

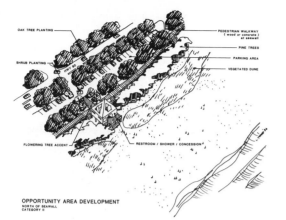

OPPORTUNITY AREA DEVELOPMENT
NORTH OF SEAWALL
CATEGORY II

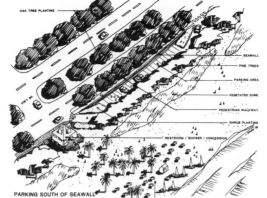

PARKING SOUTH OF SEAWALL
CATEGORY I & II

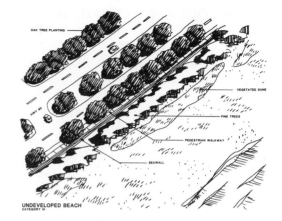

UNDEVELOPED BEACH
CATEGORY III

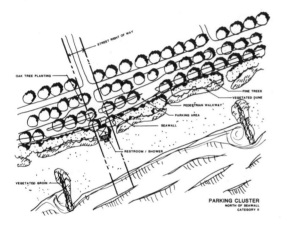

PARKING CLUSTER
NORTH OF SEAWALL
CATEGORY II

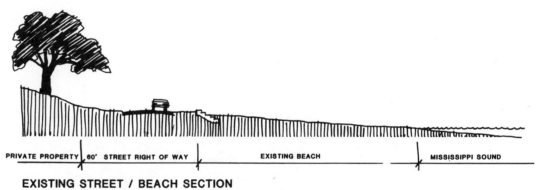

EXISTING STREET / BEACH SECTION

Before *(facing page, top left)* and after *(facing page, top center)* development of Highway 90 *(top left). Facing page, top right:* Restrooms are located within public right-of-ways, side-stepping riparian rights problems. *Center left:* Much needed parking is realized in front of the old seawall and behind the new primary dune *(top center,* and *center* and *bottom right).* Nodal developments, such as Buccaneer State Park *(facing page, bottom),* carry peak-load activities, allowing one section of the beach to remain totally undeveloped *(top right).*

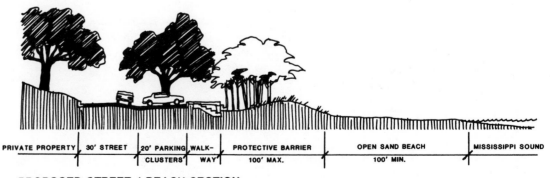

PROPOSED STREET / BEACH SECTION

PASCAGOULA WATERFRONT

A small city with a population of 30,000, located in a region of 150,000 people, Pascagoula is the center of the fishing and shipbuilding industries of Mississippi. Even though the city is surrounded on three sides by water, it maintains very little direct recreation access to it. Until the first phase of the plan's completion, there was no place to eat, drink or enjoy oneself at the water's edge. Industry had taken over the entire edge, shutting out pedestrian access. Moreover, the aesthetics of the town were represented by the ugly commercial strip and fast-food corridors, radiating a negative community image which was not conducive to tourist-oriented activities.

The plan began at the outer boundaries and moved inward. Starting with the proposed urban corridor zoning, a new community image was created through sign, landscape, land-use, and zoning ordinances. The development proposed six major "windows on the river," developments that would weave a new fabric for the city's rapport with the Pascagoula River and the Gulf of Mexico. A festival marketplace of 25,000 square feet is proposed in conjunction with a riverfront park and museum, nature center, and marina complex. Funding for the first phase came from the Community Development Block Grant Section 108 funds, which allows a community to receive several years entitlements in advance for a project of specific merit. The project's promotion of a high quality of life helped Pascagoula to be chosen as a base for a Navy home-porting fleet, which will generate revenues of $40 million per year for the city, and set in motion several development projects, using city-owned land to provide ancillary office operations to the Navy home port. The revenues from these developments will fund the Riverwalk, Maritime Center, Historic Front Street, Fisherman's Wharf and Village, and the Greenwood Island Marina Complex. All the projects are coming to life and are being funded by the Economic Development Council for the city and county and supported and directed by the Waterfront Committee of Pascagoula, an advocacy group that sponsored the original master plan and remains the force behind the plan's progress.

Project Criteria
Name: Pascagoula Waterfront
Location: Pascagoula, Mississippi
Date completed: in process
Size: 50 acres, 25,000 square feet; festival marketplace, 10,000 square feet; fisherman's village, 300-slip marina; office complex; Maritime Center

Description of Project Area Prior to Improvement
Waterfront city with no access to gulf, river, or estuary. Heavy industrial orienta-

tion placed low value on community image and recreational facilities despite the city's having the highest per capita income for the state of Mississippi.

Results of Project Completion

Jobs: 80 to 120 jobs

Tax base: $2 million to $5 million from development; $40 million from naval base

Events: Flagship Festival, Blessing of the Fleet, water parades, holiday events

Tourism increase: Shrimp Trawler Museum (in Phase I) alone is presently drawing 30,000 tourists per year; total will exceed 200,000 visitors.

Characteristics: a waterfront city returns to life at the edge.

Unique Attributes of the Project

Architecture and site: southern Mississippi vernacular; coastal ecological zone.

Theme: industrial waterfront

Basis for theme: shipbuilding and fishing village

Land use: festival marketplace, residential, industrial

Project Status

Phase I presently underway with marina complex and riverpark. Navy home port to start up in 1990. Plan took three years to implement because of industry-related environmental problems; thus it is important to start the environmental approval process as soon as possible.

Top right: The whole riverfront development starts at the roadway image, with urban corridor ordinances for landscape, signage, and zoning criteria *(bottom right).*

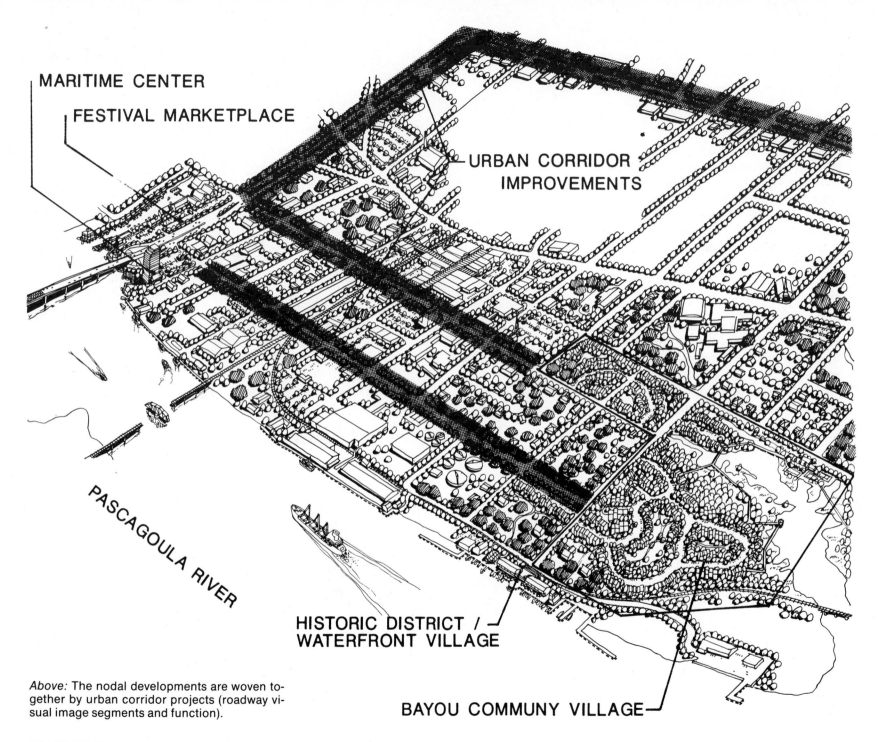

MARITIME CENTER

FESTIVAL MARKETPLACE

URBAN CORRIDOR
IMPROVEMENTS

PASCAGOULA RIVER

HISTORIC DISTRICT /
WATERFRONT VILLAGE

BAYOU COMMUNY VILLAGE

Above: The nodal developments are woven together by urban corridor projects (roadway visual image segments and function).

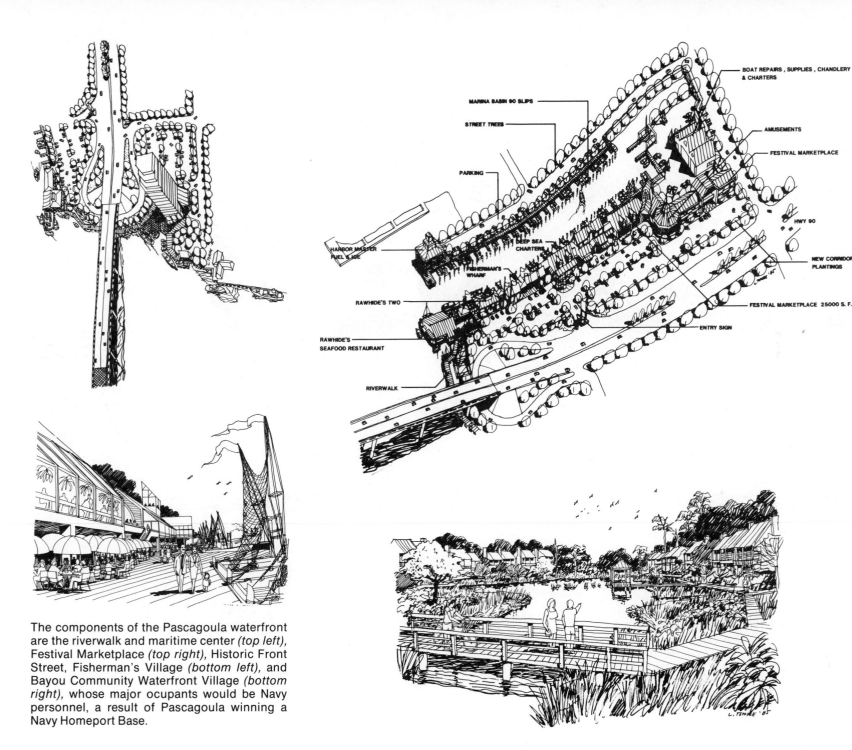

BOAT REPAIRS , SUPPLIES , CHANDLERY & CHARTERS

MARINA BASIN 90 SLIPS

STREET TREES

AMUSEMENTS

FESTIVAL MARKETPLACE

PARKING

HWY 90

NEW CORRIDOR PLANTINGS

HARBOR MASTER FUEL & ICE

DEEP SEA CHARTERS

FISHERMAN'S WHARF

FESTIVAL MARKETPLACE 25000 S. F.

RAWHIDE'S TWO

ENTRY SIGN

RAWHIDE'S SEAFOOD RESTAURANT

RIVERWALK

The components of the Pascagoula waterfront are the riverwalk and maritime center *(top left),* Festival Marketplace *(top right),* Historic Front Street, Fisherman's Village *(bottom left),* and Bayou Community Waterfront Village *(bottom right),* whose major ocupants would be Navy personnel, a result of Pascagoula winning a Navy Homeport Base.

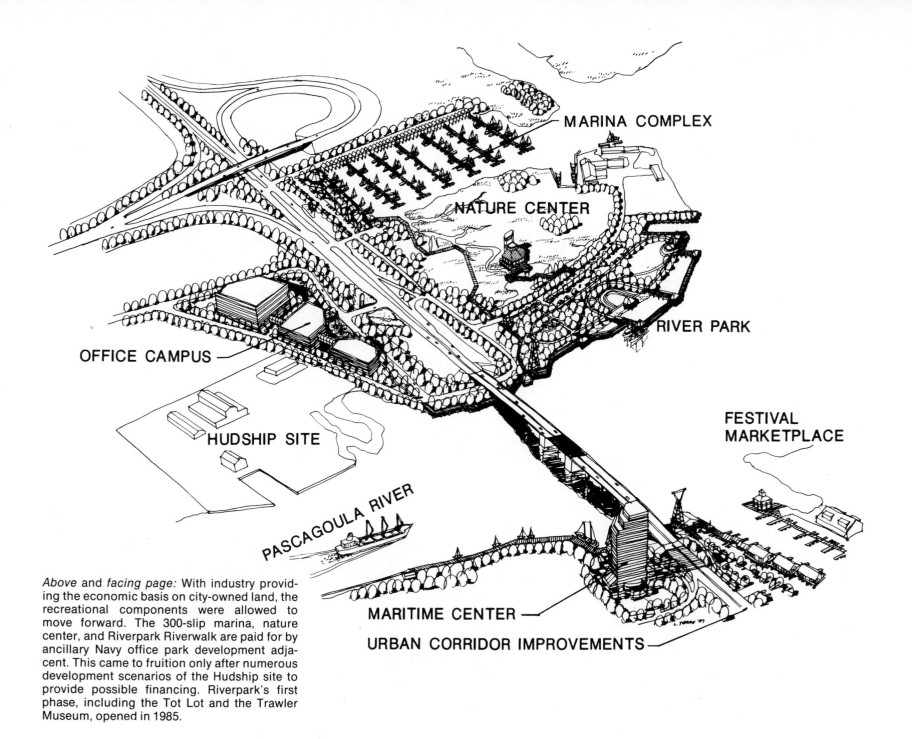

MARINA COMPLEX

NATURE CENTER

RIVER PARK

OFFICE CAMPUS

HUDSHIP SITE

FESTIVAL MARKETPLACE

PASCAGOULA RIVER

MARITIME CENTER

URBAN CORRIDOR IMPROVEMENTS

Above and *facing page:* With industry providing the economic basis on city-owned land, the recreational components were allowed to move forward. The 300-slip marina, nature center, and Riverpark Riverwalk are paid for by ancillary Navy office park development adjacent. This came to fruition only after numerous development scenarios of the Hudship site to provide possible financing. Riverpark's first phase, including the Tot Lot and the Trawler Museum, opened in 1985.

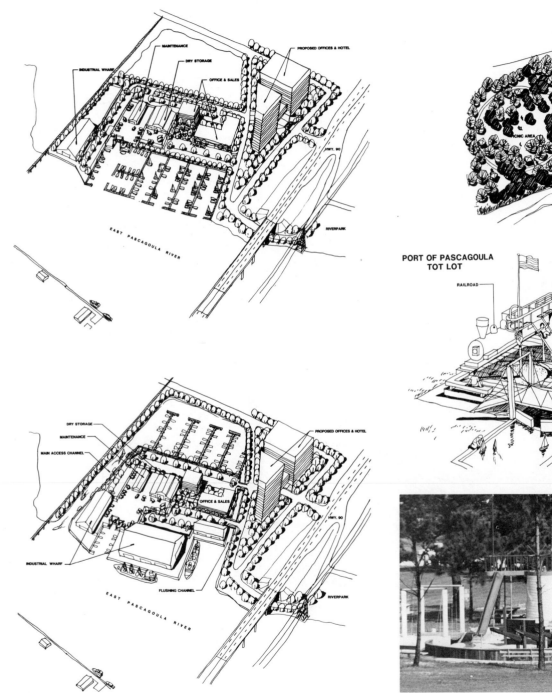

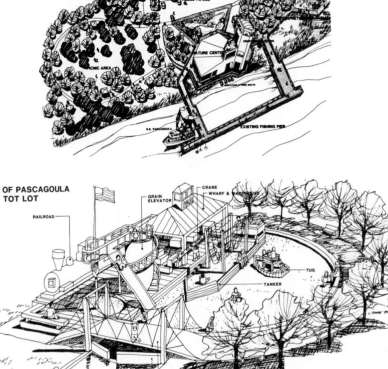

**PORT OF PASCAGOULA
TOT LOT**

Above: The maritime center and riverwalk will give Pascagoula a new image and water orientation for recreation and economic development.

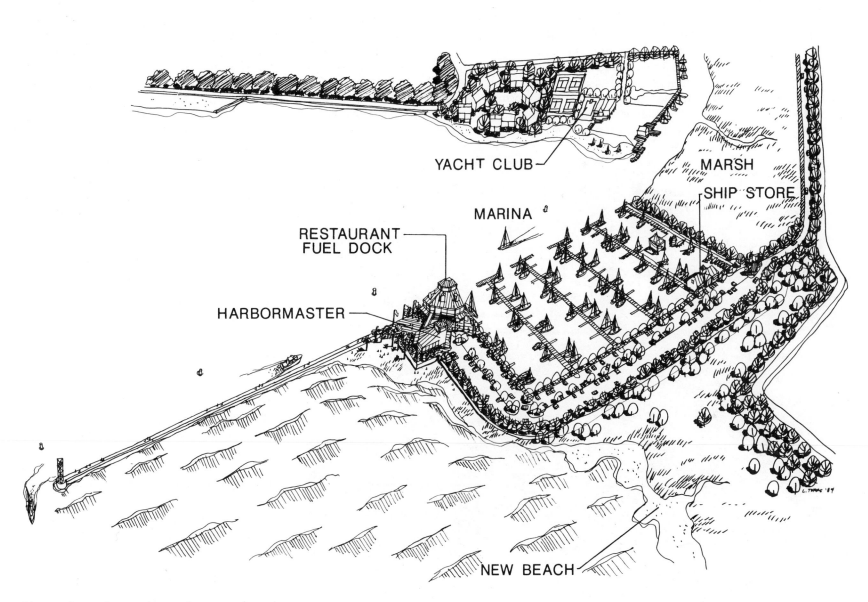

YACHT CLUB

MARSH

SHIP STORE

MARINA

RESTAURANT
FUEL DOCK

HARBORMASTER

NEW BEACH

Above: A previous scheme for a marina at Greenwood Island could not survive environmental review, even though it was adjacent to a disposal site.

SOUTHBANK RIVERWALK

With a population of 850,000, the city of Jacksonville was a substantial waterfront city without a recreational waterfront. The south bank of the Saint John's River featured some 4,000,000 square feet of office, hotel, commercial, restaurant, and recreational facilities, all without interlinkage or access to use the river's edge. Mayor Jake Godbold saw the potential in a promotional master plan produced by the firm of Cashio, Cochran, Torre/Design Consortium and proceeded to build a consensus, supporting the talents and capabilities of the Downtown Development Authority (DDA). Only three years later, the riverwalk is the most popular recreational facility and tourism asset in the entire city.

Waterfront events include boat races, boat parades, and excursions provided by water taxis and tour organizers and have encouraged cruise ships and yachts to operate from the water's edge. This expansion has extended to the riverwalk, which, with evening concerts, vendors, and the like, has become a place for people of all ages. It is hard to imagine that the annual influx of 800,000 visitors simply did not exist two years ago.

The second phase, which will represent another 11 million dollars in development, is already underway, and will complement the recently opened festival marketplace complex, art center, convention center, aquarium complex, and the addition of another tributary, McCoy's Creek. With all of these projects valued at over 55 million dollars, the city of Jacksonville now possesses a new, vibrant waterfront and the economic viability to ensure its longevity and quality of operation.

Project Criteria
Name: Southbank Riverwalk
Location: Jacksonville, Florida
Date completed: 1985
Size: 1.1 miles long; 4 million square feet office, hotel and commercial space; five restaurants, two cafes (under the bridge) 650,000 city population, metropolitan area 850,000
Cost: $6.3 million

Description of Project Area Prior to Improvement
Adjacent developments, such as service areas, parking, and the like, near industrial river edge; originally, no real orientation or pedestrian circulation feasible at the edge of the Saint John's River.

Results of Project Completion
Jobs: Over 300
Tax base: Over 2 million

Events: dinner cruises, a variety of water facilities, water taxis, cruise ship excursions, boat races and parades, concerts, and six special events per year

Tourism increase: 400,000 to 800,000 tourists per year

Characteristics: Jacksonville now thoroughly uses and enjoys the waterfront it grew from historically; now the major attraction in town

Unique Attributes of the Project

Architecture and site: contemporary elements interacting with classic nautical materials, wooden decks, and so on

Theme: a living waterfront, ship museum, and recreational facility

Basis for theme: historic development of Jacksonville at water's edge.

Land use: 125,000 square feet of festival marketplace, with 250,000 square-foot expansion to the marketplace in Phase II.

Project status

The riverwalk is presently the most popular attraction in Jacksonville, with over 7,000 tourists per average weekend day and 50,000 on event weekends. Quality control during construction phase, however, caused problems for project's image that had to be overcome. Thus, it is important in development projects that management carefully screen consultants to ensure their competancy to get the job done on time and on budget to maintain public enthusiasm.

Top right: The Mainstreet Bridge served as a major deterrent to the interconnection of the Saint John's south bank river frontage. *Facing page* and *bottom right:* The Under-the-Bridge Café sought to thematically make this linkage a major strength of the whole scheme.

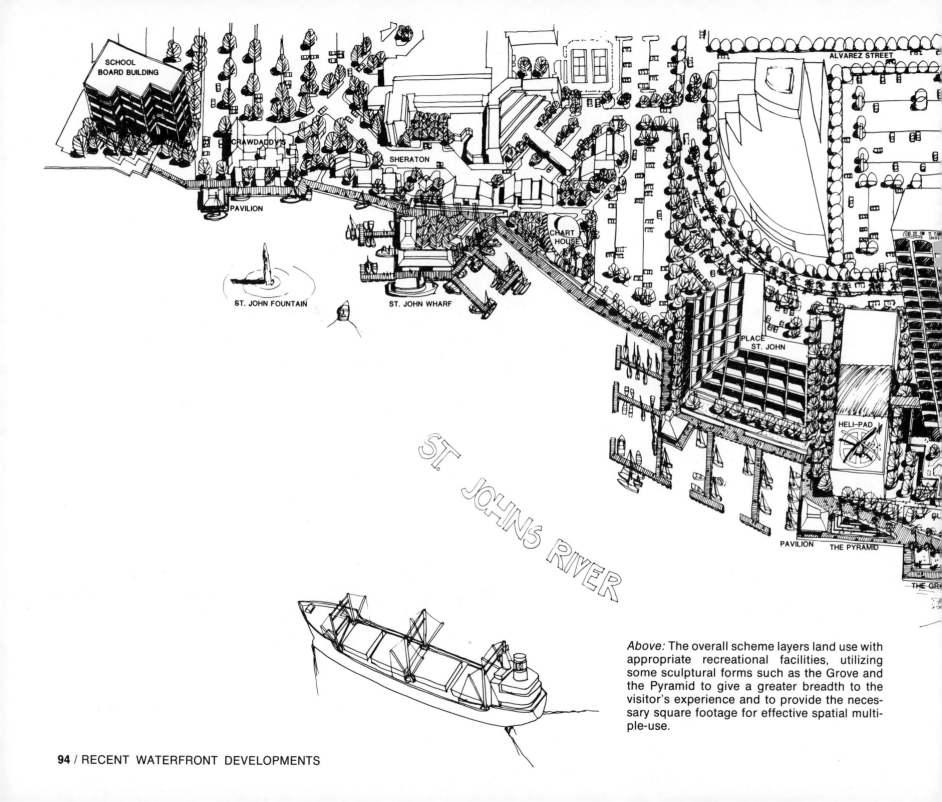

Labels within image:
SCHOOL BOARD BUILDING
CRAWDADDY'S
PAVILION
SHERATON
ST. JOHN FOUNTAIN
ST. JOHN WHARF
CHART HOUSE
ALVAREZ STREET
GULF LI
PLACE ST. JOHN
HELI-PAD
ST. JOHN'S RIVER
PAVILION   THE PYRAMID
THE GR

Above: The overall scheme layers land use with appropriate recreational facilities, utilizing some sculptural forms such as the Grove and the Pyramid to give a greater breadth to the visitor's experience and to provide the necessary square footage for effective spatial multiple-use.

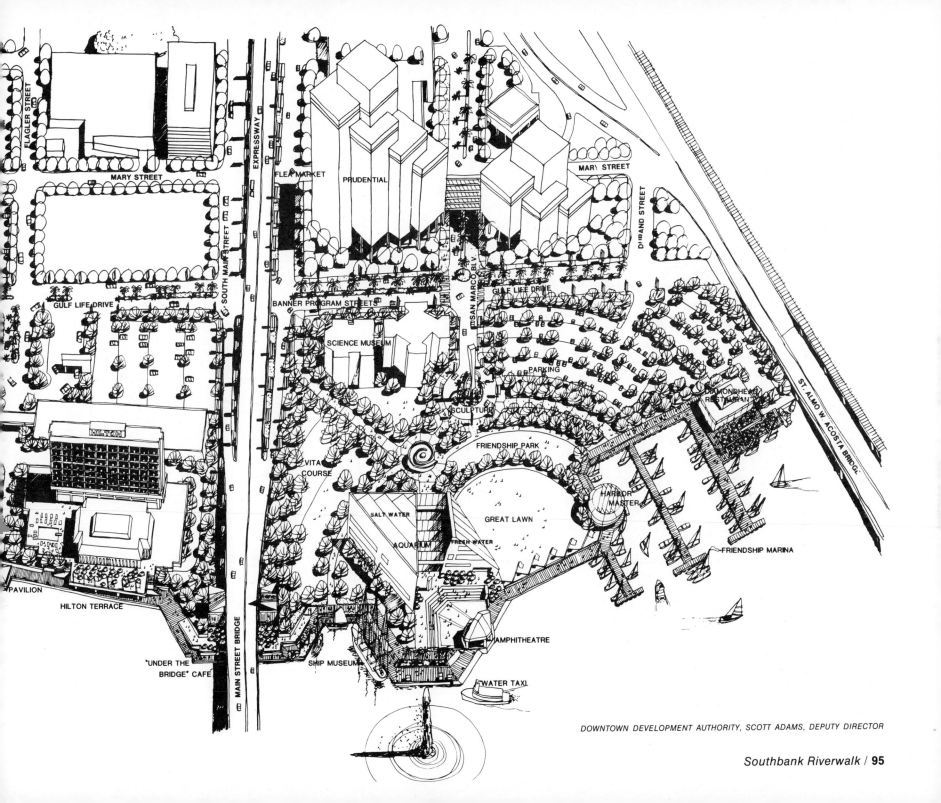

DOWNTOWN DEVELOPMENT AUTHORITY, SCOTT ADAMS, DEPUTY DIRECTOR

Top: Broad boardwalks interconnect the millions of square footage or adjacent offices, commercial, hotel, and institutional land uses *(bottom left),* while providing specialty areas such as the Fisherman's Wharf *(bottom right).* *Facing Page:* The success of the development has been phenomenal, with an annual attendance of just under one million, after being open for only two years. The river was previously devoid of pleasure craft.

Top left: Pavilions were designed for multiple use, from picnics to symphony concerts, and are properly lit with neon for nighttime use.

Top right: With an average width of 35 feet, the project has functioned well even during the opening celebration attendance of 50,000 people. *Bottom left* and *right:* Weekday attendance is allowed a far more spacious setting.

Facing page: The Under-the-Bridge-Café, with pavilions, water-wall fountains, and ramps at left.

PETER FOE/FOTOWORKS

BAYSHORE BOULEVARD

Bayshore Boulevard has often been considered the single most important image maker of Tampa, Florida. In terms of function, however, it is little more than a scenic drive for motorists or a jogging path for recreational use. Based on the city's desire to create a special waterfront for its historic waterfront city, a comprehensive plan was requested to produce more recreational and water-oriented opportunities, ones that would be able to finance capital improvements and to become self-sufficient in operation. At the same time, a new festival marketplace had opened the 65,000-square-foot Harbour Island, several new office buildings were underway on the Hillsborough River, and a new convention center was being developed in the waterfront. All of this marked a decided return to the Tampa Bay waterfront, which had been unidentified since the decline in the importation of Cuban cigar tobacco by ship.

Out of the project's 5.5-mile length, three nodal developments were designed, providing over 200 marina slips, a new aquatic center, and a proposed Gasparilla Cultural and Heritage Museum. (Gasparilla Day is roughly the equivalent of Mardi Gras in New Orleans and the day on which "pirates" seize the city from the waterfront. A new proposal for an aquarium linked to the Hillsborough Riverwalk would complete the waterfront development. The Boulevard project's economic development would be based on increment tax financing in addition to pro-formaed waterfront activities and services such as the River Café and the Transportation Center, from which visitors could take a river cruise upstream on the Hillsborough River to the newly renovated Lowry Park Zoological Garden. This networking of facilities will provide a tremendous family-attraction base for these and other facilities linked to Bayshore Boulevard. This project will represent a total waterfront development that will prove itself economically important to Tampa's growing reputation as "America's Next Great City."

Project Criteria

Name: Bayshore Boulevard Development
Location: Tampa, Florida
Date completed: in process (projected completion, 1990)
Size: 5 linear miles; city population 600,000; regional population 1.4 million
Cost: $51 million

Description of Project Area Prior to Improvement

Major scenic drive in Tampa, located on Tampa Bay but with no access to the water other than view. Extreme shortage of marina slips, recreation facilities, parking, and economic development.

Results of Project Completion

Jobs: 200
Tax base: boat parades and races, Gasparilla Festival, waterfront activities, holiday events, concerts
Tourism increase: 1 million anticipated with aquarium, Harbour Island development, and waterfront nodes.
Characteristics: increased access and regional use of the key image-making corridor of Tampa.

Top right: At Tampa's major waterfront corridor, the pedestrian is put perilously close to vehicular traffic and even seating turrets *(bottom right)* force the view toward traffic, not the bay.

Unique Attributes of the Project

Architecture and site: southern Florida vernacular, boardwalks, and waterfront details
Theme: orientation toward boating activities
Basis for theme: linkage to Tampa's history as a port city
Land use: commercial, office, festival marketplace, residential, recreational, convention center

Project Status

Bayshore Boulevard development is in progress as is the convention center. Harbour Island with festival marketplace is experiencing a slow start-up but appears to have long-term viability. The location of the aquarium will underpin the necessary waterfront attractions, which will lead into the final riverwalk phase of the riverwalk, similar to that at Jacksonville.

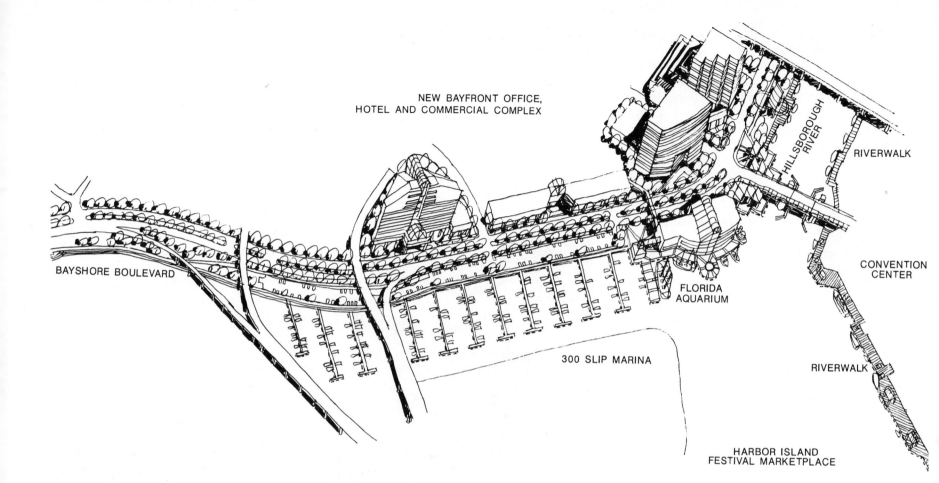

NEW BAYFRONT OFFICE,
HOTEL AND COMMERCIAL COMPLEX

HILLSBOROUGH RIVER

RIVERWALK

BAYSHORE BOULEVARD

FLORIDA AQUARIUM

CONVENTION CENTER

300 SLIP MARINA

RIVERWALK

HARBOR ISLAND
FESTIVAL MARKETPLACE

Above: Nodal developments proposed for the downtown area show much-needed marina slips, and an aquarium and riverwalk to complement the in-process convention center and Harbour Island development.

Giving greater visual emphasis to the entry sequence onto Bayshore Boulevard *(facing page, bottom left)* creates a greater sense of importance *(facing page, top left)* while a stepped gabion system repairs the existing seawall at one-quarter of the cost, providing two protection systems and access to the water's edge for the first time *(facing page, top* and *bottom right).*

Left: A proposed central node within the five-mile project length is proposed for an aquatic center and museum. *Top right:* The gabion system gives access to the water while it was not previously allowed *(bottom right).*

BRUCE FORRESTER

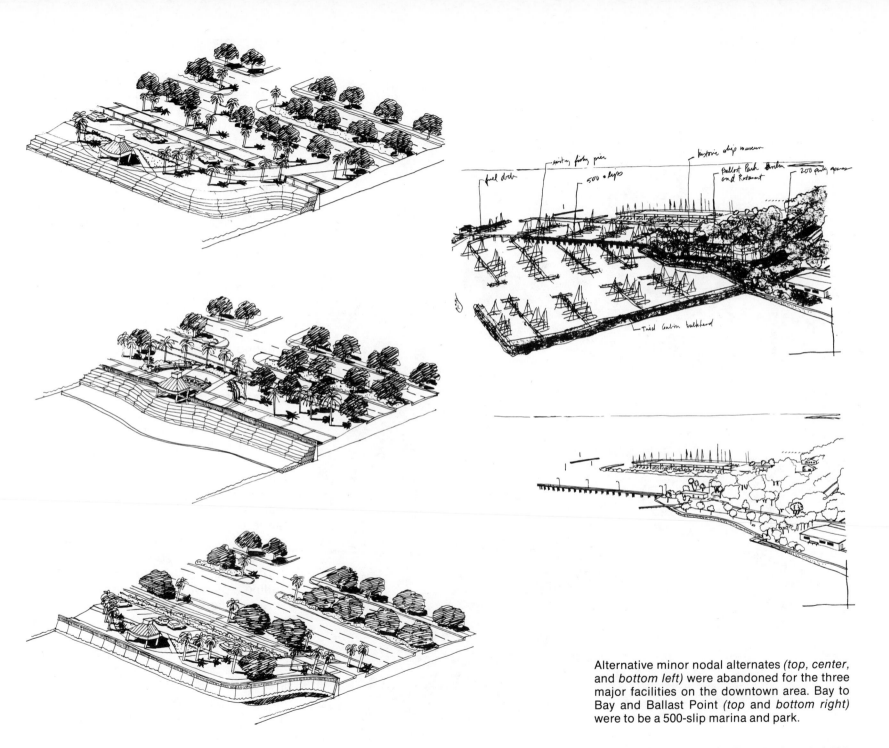

fuel dock
existing fishing pier
500 slips
historic ship museum
Ballast Park Pavilion and Restaurant
200 parking spaces
Tied Gabion bulkhead

Alternative minor nodal alternates *(top, center, and bottom left)* were abandoned for the three major facilities on the downtown area. Bay to Bay and Ballast Point *(top and bottom right)* were to be a 500-slip marina and park.

PORT GRIMAUD

Carved out of a lowland adjacent to the azure waters of the Mediterranean Sea is the French sailing village of Port Grimaud. Its image is similar to that of Venice in terms of both scale and texture, except that automobile access is possible to the multiple peninsulae that project into the man-made water basin. Perhaps the single most important image-making feature of the development is the barrel-tile roof and textured stucco-wall construction, reiterating the vernacular of southern France. With a variety of setbacks, these units exhibit both zero lot frontage and parklike edges with trees and lush plantings. The development's height is limited to no more than four stories, successfully creating a human-scale village with an influx of tourists so great that it is now one of the most celebrated and visited developments in France.

Francois Spoerry of Cabinet Spoerry in Mulhouse, France, acknowledges that the concept of the development was derived from a reconstruction of a prehistoric lagoon city that he observed as a child at the Landsmuseum in Zurich. It is also notable that Port Grimaud resembles the fabric of the historic waterfront community of Milneburg in New Orleans (see pages 62–63) built some 3,000 years later.

The initial sketches for the development outline a plan for a community that could "live" at the water's edge, a city that, although accessible by car, could function without interruption from its service and access arterials. Port Grimaud's many bridges add the romance and scale found in precedents from Venice to San Antonio. Many dollars were saved in the construction phases by using "dry" procedures, excavating lagoons and using the fill for the adjacent site work and parking areas. The marina, as designed, would probably not be permitted to be built in the United States because of poor flushing capability, a flaw that has resulted in the construction of contemporary marinas with flush-box culverts, permeable breakwaters, and large mitigation banks of grasses forming natural barriers to wave energy. In spite of any drawbacks, Port Grimaud is as handsome and romantic a community as could be imagined—certainly the basis for its continued success.

Project Criteria

Name: Port Grimaud
Location: Grimaud, France
Date completed: begun 1966; in process
Size: 189 acres containing 1,871 residential units (2,271 when complete)
Cost: over $65 million construction costs to date

Description of Project Area Prior to Improvement

The first 70 acres which were acquired in 1962 were part of a low-lying bog land at the mouth of a river, the Giscle, on the Bay of Saint Tropez. The only attempt to utilize this marshland had been a short lived sand and gravel operation.

Results of Project Completion

Jobs: over 300 permanent jobs
Tax base: exceeds the tax base of the town of Grimaud, which is the government seat of the community that includes Port Grimaud. The permit to begin this project took four years to obtain.
Events: various festivals, boat races, concerts

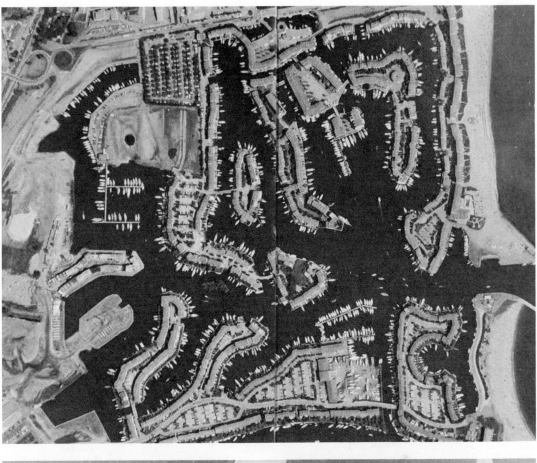

Tourism increase: Port Grimaud is the second most visited attraction in France after the Eiffel Tower and on a par with Mont-Saint-Michel with over 1 million visitors each year.

Characteristics: this popular resort provides year-round living, with shops, restaurants, a shipyard, a church, and many other amenities.

Unique Attributes of the Project

Architecture and site: the architecture and the scale of the existing Mediterranean villages

Theme: a waterfront village such as Port Merion in Wales, or Venice in Italy

Basis for theme: waterfront life-style and scale of southern France

Land use: mixed use

Project Status

The success is based on workable scale, theme, and image, which promotes a highly romantic waterfront life-style.

Drawing on his memories from a museum of a prehistoric lagoon city *(top left)* (which looks more like the result in New Orleans' Milneburg) Spoerry's drawings *(bottom left)* seem more akin to Venice.

Carved from a coastal lowland *(facing page, top left)* utilizing dry-construction technology and flooding the canals later *(facing page, bottom left)*, the development comes to life with its many places, bridges, and its romantic serpentine canal *(facing page, top right)*.

COSTA SMERALDA

The beautiful granite coast of the hardy Italian island of Sardinia, sculpted by wind and water, serves as the backdrop for one of the most beautiful resorts in the Mediterranean Sea—Costa Smeralda. Developed by the Consorzio Costa Smeralda, headed by the Aga Khan, the project has been in existence for less than fifteen years, yet it has become one of the major resorts in the world.

Unlike that of Port Grimaud, this development is more of a hill town adjacent to a waterfront project—resembling Positano or Portofino. High-energy waves also control the design and layout of the Porto Cervo marina and boating facilities, but these winds, which frequently blow at more than 30 knots for two weeks at a time, form the character of a waterfront community engrossed in sailing. Already the Sardinia Cup has become one of the premier sailing races in the world. This event, along with museums, exhibitions, festivals, road races, concerts, tennis matches, and a variety of recreational activities, has created a unique community for work and play within the Sardinian environment. With a tourist season spanning less than eight months, the development is transformed from a dormant winter community to a lively and vibrant city overnight as the weather warms, generally in June.

The centerpiece of the development is Porto Cervo, the new yachting center.

The sweeping arc of the marina complex *(left)* follows the geometry of the adjacent hill *(facing page, top right)* while allowing the marina full flexibility in moorage variety *(facing page, bottom right)*.

When it was proposed originally, the marina met with opposition as adjacent villa owners felt that it would be an intrusion, especially with the marina maintenance facility. The designers felt that it would actually be the opposite situation, reminiscent of the Portofino and Caglieri waterfronts, where the beauty of sailing vessels both in and out of the water could be observed. This complete concept of a marina was the basis of the layout and development of the facilities, with new residential units created to include integrated boat storage and maintenance facilities for the owner. The marina now houses an impressive fleet of 12-meter racing yachts with their own hydraulic cradles, which has provided the waterfront with a new level of excitement in yachting activities.

Project Criteria
Name: Costa Smeralda
Location: Sardinia, Italy
Date completed: in process
Size: 75 linear miles of coastline on the island of Sardinia, developed by the Consorzio Costa Smeralda
Cost: Over $100 million

Description of Project Area Prior to Improvement
Beautiful, rugged granite coastline on the island of Sardinia, agricultural activities and animal herding prevail as land use.

Results of Project Completion
Jobs: over 1,000
Tax base: not available
Events: Sardinia Cup, boat races, off-road auto racing, holiday events, festivals
Tourism increase: now one of the most popular resorts in the world

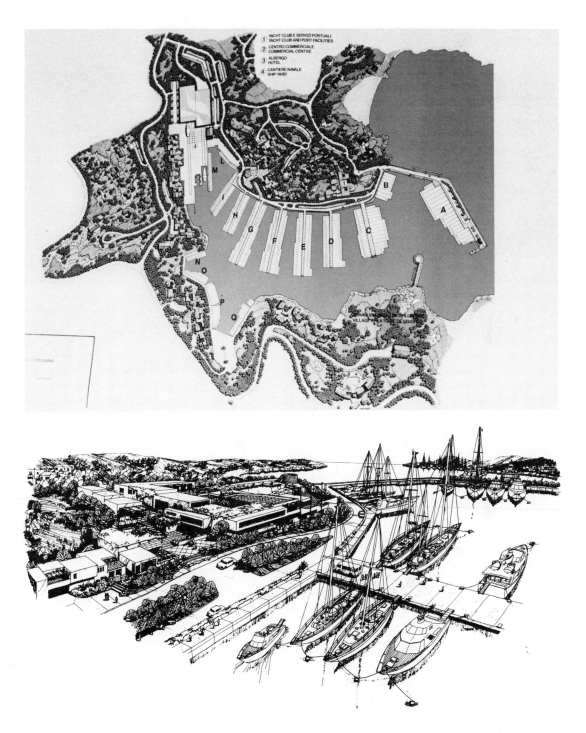

Early drawings of the complex sought to explore the massing relationship between water's edge and the adjacent village *(top left* and *top, center,* and *bottom right).* The plan as realized represents a successful insertion of development *(bottom left)* into this ruggedly beautiful terrain.

Characteristics: development of area into five communities, Porto Cervo as the centerpiece, created a waterfront community with access to some of Italy's most beautiful water.

Unique Attributes of the Project

Architecture and site: Sardinian vernacular of stone walls, tile roofs, stucco and whitewashed finishes

Theme: Sardinia waterfront community

Basis for theme: Strong fishing and waterfront life-style heritage

Land use: commercial; specialty, residential; minimal office facilities; boat facilities, including dry storage and repair.

Project Status

The development continues to grow and develop new cluster community centers. The major problem was working out a compromise with the local community to allow the development to move forward. An integral part of this compromise was the allocation of 30 percent green space for public use throughout the development.

Architectural vernacular varies from Porto Cervo *(top right)* to Cala de Volpe *(bottom left)* but yields a distinctly Mediterranean fabric *(bottom right).*

WORLD FINANCIAL CENTER: BATTERY PARK CITY PLAZA

CESAR AND PELLI AND ASSOCIATES

This waterfront complex is supported by a dense network of office, residential, and commercial facilities, totaling more than 8,000,000 square feet. Located on reclaimed river-bottom land in the Hudson River, this particular part of the overall development covers less than 20 percent of the entire acreage. The waterfront is consistent with current lower Manhattan development in terms of style and land use, but with plazas and broad walkways, allows for an orientation toward the river. A unique component is the Winter Garden, which permits year-round activities in a climate-controlled glass-vaulted environment utilizing the river as a backdrop. The plaza was the result of close collaboration among Cesar Pelli (architect), Siah Armajani and Scott Burton (public artists), and Paul Friedberg (landscape architect).

The 3.5-acre waterfront plaza at Battery Park City's World Financial Center is the first major public plaza on the Hudson River and the key element of the new Battery Park City's public areas and open space. This plaza was not conceived as an independent entity, but as a part of a continuum along the 1.5-mile waterfront esplanade. The Battery Park City Plaza has been designed to provide for the many needs of a varied group of users—from the tourist who makes a one-time visit, to the office worker who eats lunch there regularly. Consequently, the plaza is not a single-feature design, but a coordinated series of eight unified but distinct spaces. As an ensemble, they are oriented toward the buildings. They will provide a range of open spaces for the individual, for intimate groups, and for large public gatherings.

Project Criteria

Name: World Financial Center: Battery Park City Plaza

Location: Manhattan, New York

Date completed: estimation 1988

Size: 8 million square feet of buildings; 3.5-acre plaza

Cost: $1.5 billion

Description of Project Area Prior to Improvement

Landfill in location of old piers; originally master plan of 1960s redone in 1978 by Cooper-Eckstut. Cesar Pelli received commission based on competition, which used new master plan as part of competition guidelines.

Results of Project Completion

Jobs: not available

Tax base: not available

Events: increased waterfront access and activity

Tourism increase: not available

Characteristics: better access to Hudson River and water front

Unique Attributes of the Project

Architecture and site: high-density urban fabric created on landfill

Theme: World Financial Center

Basis for theme: land uses adjacent and contained

Fan Pier accomplishes what the World Financial Center did not; it creates a city within a city with an incredible variety of waterfront scale *(facing page)* and use. The romantic and pragmatic aspects of the development successfully succeeded in creating what will be one of the nation's best developments *(top* and *bottom right).*

CESAR AND PELLI AND ASSOCIATES

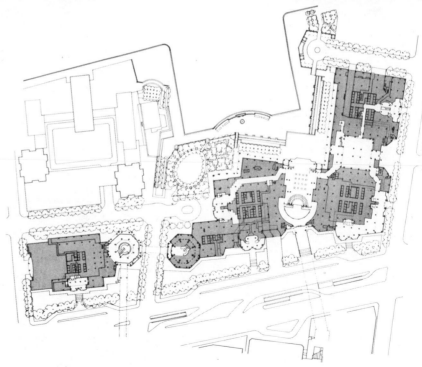

CESAR AND PELLI AND ASSOCIATES

FAN PIER MASTER PLAN

The Fan Pier master plan calls for the development of 18.5 acres on Boston Harbor, an 806-room Hyatt Regency Hotel, 1.3 million gross square feet of office and commercial space; an 80-slip marina, and below-grade parking for 2,500 cars occupying piers 1, 2, and 3 in South Boston. A central element of the design is a proposed 83-foot wide navigable canal, oriented to frame views of the historic Custom House Tower and lined with shops and restaurants. The canal's walls will be faced with granite block salvaged from the site. Pedestrian and vehicular bridges across the canal will extend neighborhood streets and the planned Harbor Park promenade into the site.

The plan creates over three acres of landscaped public space and pedestrian walks. A public park will overlook the waterfront and downtown Boston, and a promenade extending Boston's Harbor Park will wrap the perimeter of the project along the harbor edge and both sides of the canal.

This canal and proposed marina are the key image makers for the entire project, and by bringing water into the site, they create a true waterfront community using the Venice/Grimaud theme but at a much more urban scale. Particularly successful is the project's relationship to Boston's city fabric and the linkage of the city to the entire waterfront. An environmentally critical asset provided by the canal's linkage to the marina basin is excellent flushing, important in preventing the basin from becoming septic.

Additional elements of the plan feature a 47-story brick and granite tower hotel on the harbor, with a low-rise base containing the lobby and all public spaces. Three ground-level restaurants will front on the canal, marina, and harbor; a rooftop restaurant will offer spectacular views of downtown Boston and the waterfront. South of the canal will be four office and retail buildings—ranging from 10 to 26 stories—and a public and cultural affairs facility providing exhibition and performance space. Three residential buildings offering over 500 dwelling units will be located north of the canal adjacent to the hotel.

Project Criteria

Name: Fan Pier Master Plan
Location: Boston
Date completed: 1995 (projected)
Size: 18.5 site acres/3 million building square feet
Cost: $735 million

Description of Project Area Prior to Improvement

On-grade parking, empty land, and several storage sheds

Results of Project Completion

Jobs: 7,600 permanent jobs; 2,300 construction jobs
Tax base: real estate taxes: $12.0 million
   hotel: $2.8 million
   food and beverage: $1.3 million
   retail sales tax: $2.5 million

Total $18.6 million
Tourism increase: 10,000 people per day includes visitors, workers, and residents
Characteristics: new mixed-use area of the city; an inaccessible, blighted area opened up for public recreation, commerce, and living.

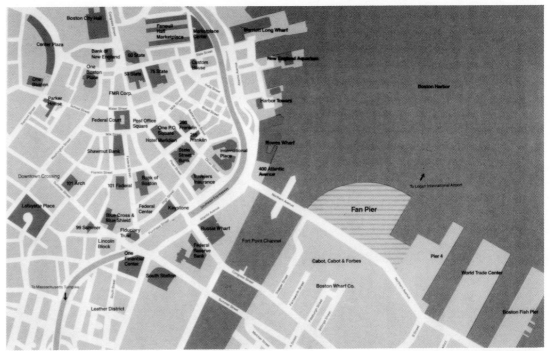

CESAR AND PELLI AND ASSOCIATES

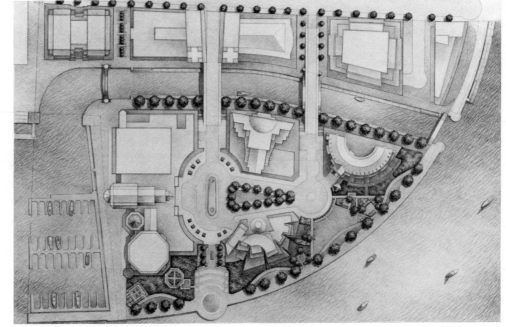

CESAR AND PELLI AND ASSOCIATES

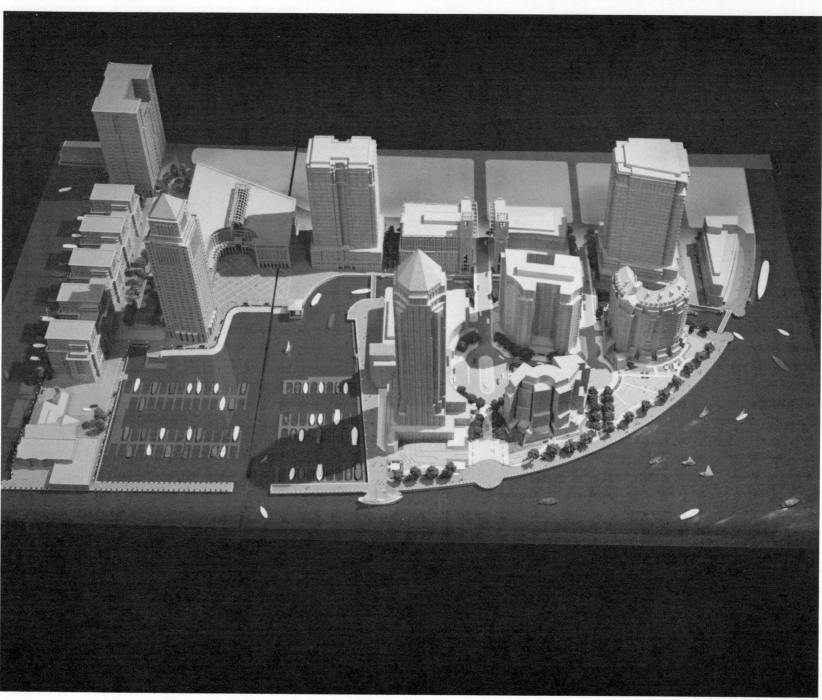

Unique Attributes of the Project

Architecture and site: introduction of a retail/pedestrian promenade along a new canal; 60 percent public open space (100 percent barrier free). a variety of architects working within a comprehensive plan.

Theme: a natural extension of the city, with emphasis on a clear sequence of public spaces and the development of a variety of urban waterfront experiences.

Basis for theme: to take advantage of the unique waterfront site and the architectural urban character of Boston.

Land use: 800-room banquet hotel; 550 market-rate and affordable housing units; 1.4 million square feet of office space; 150,000 square feet of retail space; public and cultural affairs facility; marina; below-grade parking; public park and promenades

Project Status

Project is presently under review by the BRA for schematic design approval.

STEVE ROSENTHAL

STEVE ROSENTHAL

SEASIDE, FLORIDA

This residential development makes use of the traditional small-town urban forms of northwestern Florida (narrow streets, contained squares, and the like) and the continuation of the local vernacular building tradition through the Seaside Urban Code, which has produced a coherent and cohesive townscape. Although the houses are all different from one another they share a common vocabulary of forms and materials. Houses in this part of he country are raised above the ground, to enable breezes to flow under the structure. They have ample windows and fairly deep roof overhangs to allow for good cross ventilation, even in the rain, and porches are oriented to catch the summer breezes from the sea and provide shade from the high summer sun while still permitting the low winter sun to warm the house. All houses are required to have front porches and picket fences, the latter to help strengthen the spatial definition of the street and the former, along with practical reasons, to help create a sense of neighborliness. The front porches are a comfortable conversational distance from the street, and conversations between porch sitters and strollers are a common occurence.

Seaside's beach is not walled off from the rest of the community, and its streets and squares are generally filled with people walking and children playing. The town itself is compact and fairly high density and is thus very sparing in its use of land. Seaside's Urban Code requires the retention of native landscape and prohibits lawns, resulting in an absence of noisy lawnmowers and a significant saving of water, fertilizers, and pesticides.

Project Criteria

Name: Seaside
Location: on the Gulf of Mexico, Walton County, Florida
Date completed: 1999 (projected)
Size: 2,300 linear frontage in process on the Gulf of Mexico
Costs: not available

Description of Project Area Prior to Improvement

Secondary dune and scrub vegetation adjacent to the Gulf of Mexico and beach area. Flanked on either side by conventional condominiums and townhouse developments, which have recently experienced marketing problems.

Results of Project Completion

Jobs: 150 construction averge; 72 in related services and sales areas
Tax base: property taxes of $2 million per year for residential and commercial properties
Events: summer movie series, theatrical productions, fall chamber music series, fairs, street dance performances, and benefits for local institutions
Tourism increase: substantial recent increase
Characteristics: Seaside has attempted to demonstrate that life at the beach can be far more pleasant in a wood-frame house with porches and cross ventilation, than in an air-conditioned condominium unit, even though the house does not have a picture window view of the beach. Also, by placing the houses fairly close together and by making driving relatively inconvenient and walking very pleasant, developers have tried to show the delights of a pedestrian community.

Unique Attributes of the Project

Architecture and site: northwestern Florida
Theme: re-creation of traditional town urban form of the 1930s and 1940s
Basis for theme: historically appropriate to northern Florida
Land use: development will contain 350 single-family houses, 200 apartment houses, 200 hotel rooms, 50,000 square feet of retail space, 20,000 square feet of office space, and public buildings such as a town hall/conference center, library, church, tennis and swim club, beach pavilions, gazebos, garden structures, and so on.

Below: Romance prevails, underpinned by logical pragmatism, with a return to the 1940 seaside vernacular with natural ventilation.

Project Status

Seaside is enjoying a phenomenal marketing success in an area in which condominiums are practically unsalable. It has also developed successful neighborhoods in which homeowners appear to share a strong pride of place. The provision of parking facilities may prove to be a problem, however. Seaside has managed to provide adequate parking according to currently accepted ratios, but its very appeal may be turning it into an "attraction," and facilities may be overloaded as a result. Developers are currently exploring the option of underground parking for the town center. Alleyways (a secondary street system) can absorb a large number of cars. In fact, it is becoming a truism that good urban planning should start with a high ratio of linear feet of street to square feet of building.

SEATTLE HARBORFRONT

Seattle has maintained a special relationship with its waterfront since the 1850s. The unique climate and the beautiful Puget Sound form the foundation for a usable waterfront to which few can compare, carved into its present shape by the trading economy. After local inhabitants had been separated from its waterfront by railroads, the Alaskan Viaduct served to further separate access by allowing the automobile to dominate the water's edge. Ironically, this elevated structure, which divided the city from its waterfront, today actually helps provide needed parking space adjacent to the waterfront development.

Building on the fact that many of the piers already provide festival marketplace activites, a successful (if small) aquarium, and recreational facilities, Harborfront is a concerted attempt to make a good waterfront an excellent one. The development plan proposes needed marina space along the downtown waterfront (heretofore missing), new restaurants, retail and office complexes, and a cruise-ship terminal as well as expanded recreational facilities. A waterfront streetcar and water taxis would amplify the existing ferryboat service, giving a more animated sense to waterfront facilities and creating linkages to other historic nodal centers of Seattle's city fabric. Of all the elements, the new marina slips will yield the highest new level of functioning, from boat races to related repair services, the availability of boat launches, and other activities that had previously been enjoyed only on the lakes and interconnecting channels. The Harborfront project will unify thematically an exciting new waterfront for a city whose history and economic development have always been linked to the Puget Sound.

Project Criteria
Name: Harborfront
Location: Seattle, Washington
Date completed: in process
Size: not available
Cost: $30 million

Description of Project Area Prior to Improvement
Partially renovated waterfront with shops, restaurants, and active ferry service and boat tours. Total area lacking unity; several parts not renovated; no public marina. Aquarium facility small and expansion needed. Potential for a new cruise-ship terminal had to be analyzed, along with the need for public moorage on a very active waterfront.

Results of Project Completion
Jobs: not available
Tax base: not available
Events: numerous festivals, concerts, and special recreational programs
Tourism increase: substantial
Characteristics: increased waterfront activities, greater tourism base

Facing page: A city separated from its waterfront by an elevated expressway, Seattle has adapted well to providing a comprehensive recreational experience.

Right: The Seattle aquarium and waterfront park.

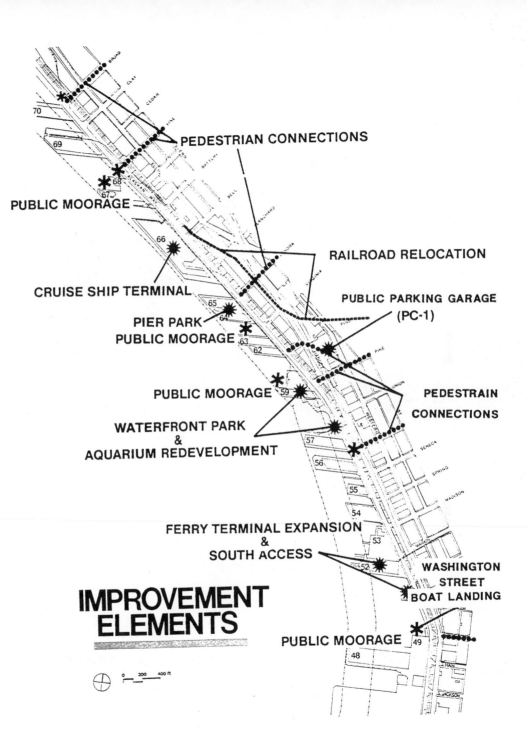

PEDESTRIAN CONNECTIONS

PUBLIC MOORAGE

RAILROAD RELOCATION

CRUISE SHIP TERMINAL

PUBLIC PARKING GARAGE (PC-1)

PIER PARK
PUBLIC MOORAGE

PUBLIC MOORAGE

PEDESTRAIN CONNECTIONS

WATERFRONT PARK
&
AQUARIUM REDEVELOPMENT

FERRY TERMINAL EXPANSION
&
SOUTH ACCESS

WASHINGTON STREET BOAT LANDING

IMPROVEMENT ELEMENTS

PUBLIC MOORAGE

0   200   400 ft

Unique Attributes of the Project

Architecture and site: rehabilitation of unique Seattle waterfront wharf vernacular

Theme: northwestern waterfront and the Puget Sound

Basis for theme: geographic and climatic

Land use: commerical, office, festival marketplace, seafood market, residential, industrial, transportation

Project Status

The waterfront is presently a success. With completion of harborfront it will become one of the premier waterfront developments in the United States.

The attempt of the city to make a good waterfront great is admirable *(above),* with major new nodal developments creating more activities *(center* and *bottom left)* and opportunities for multiple use and economic development *(facing page).*

PIER 39, SAN FRANCISCO

In a city of discriminating shoppers and diners—and in one with a long-established, popular waterfront development such as Fisherman's Wharf—the unprecedented success of Pier 39 is notable. This waterfront development, created in the early 1970s, is both self-contained and broad-based and continues to draw more visitors every year.

By appropriating the formerly underutilized pier and using salvaged materials, developers gave the new structures a warmth and patina which helps to unify the entire complex. The 730-foot pier's narrow width allows for double-loading two levels of shops, connected overhead by pedestrian bridges, which permit a comprehensive flow of traffic. The surrounding marina serves both as a dramatic backdrop and exciting waterfront use. A problem in the opening days of the marina was the use of the floating tire breakwater. Save yourself the trouble of ever using this device, as none have been successful in their operation to date. Other than the replacement of the floating tire breakwater in the marina, the overall development has held up well and continues to offer more activities and services for the community each year. The entry plaza and waterfront park create a distinct image and, through the use of proper sizing, have encouraged multiple use on a daily as well as seasonal basis.

One of the best waterfront developments in existence, Pier 39 had to compete *(left)* with the long-established Fisherman's Wharf complex nearby. Thematic entertainment and facilities such as the high-diving shows *(facing page, top right)* and full-service marina, and a proper tenant mix, underpinned the project's diversity *(facing page, bottom right).*

Project Criteria

Name: Pier 39
Location: San Francisco, California
Date completed: 1978
Size: 200,000 square feet
Cost: $54 million

Description of Project Area Prior to Improvement

Underutilized pier on San Francisco waterfront in proximity to the popular Fisherman's Wharf complex and the downtown core.

Results of Project Completion

Jobs: 2,000 full-time employees
Tax base: $4 million in revenue to the city of San Francisco.
Events: continuous—ranging from theatrical and mime performances to festivals, boat tours, carousel, shopping, and holiday celebrations
Tourism increase: 10 million visitors per year
Characteristics: an active, vibrant seaport taking visitors out over the San Francisco Bay

Unique Attributes of the Project

Architecture and site: built on an abandoned pier of existing wood from wharfs reused in new buildings to create an urban waterfront
Themes: wharf structures that would create a total environment for recreational facilities reiterative of the scale and texture of the old wharf
Basis for theme: historic precedent
Land use: commercial, festival market place, entertainment, retail

Project Status

One of the most visited facilities in California.

BRUCE FORRESTER

BRUCE FORRESTER

BRUCE FORRESTER

Facing page: The authenticity is effective with tour boats, and pleasure and industrial craft actively navigating the bay.

Right: The entry plaza is decorated to celebrate the seasons, while the basic armature of pageantry prevails year long *(top left).* The antique carousel *(bottom left)* is a major new attraction.

SANTA CRUZ BOARDWALK

As a classic example of the seaside amusement park, Santa Cruz Boardwalk exists as a success largely because of the community's strong dedication to preservation. Built during the early 1900s, the park has escaped the fate of most such simpler attractions, which suffered with the development of huge amusement centers such as Disneyworld. The success of the boardwalk is based on its continued provision of diversified recreational activities and a broadening of facilities (meeting and conference centers, food courts, and so on, which allows the development to compete for the recreational user's time with other newer, more complex, amusement parks.

The water's edge—in this case a mile long sand beach—and the numerous shoreside activities underpin the development. A shortcoming is that the main "street" is located within a double-loaded corridor of structures, rather than being situated so as to take advantage of the Pacific Ocean as a continuous backdrop. This perhaps is partly because of the tremendous force of the Pacific Ocean's waves, which prevent the extensive development of the beach area. No oceanfront is subject to waves with a longer fetch and, consequently, to greater storm damage. At the same time the drama of this beachfront is commensurate with its struggle to survive.

Project Criteria

Name: Santa Cruz Boardwalk
Location: Santa Cruz, California
Date completed: recent renovations in 1980s on 1907 original development
Size: not available
Cost: not available over $10 million in recent renovations

Description to Project Area Prior to Improvement

California coastline amusement park; developed during city's early history, very successful in 1920, fell into disrepair in the 1960's, recently renovated.

Results of Project Completion

Jobs: 400 to 1,100 employees (according to seasonal use)
Tax base: not available
Events: Clam Chowder Cook-Off, festivals, holiday celebrations, concerts, boat races, amusement rides, and shows
Tourism increase: 1.5 million tourists per year
Characteristics: tourist amusement park is a destination for many people within radius of 100 miles

Unique Attributes of the Project

Architecture and site: classic period architecture and historic amusement park vernacular
Theme: pleasure park
Basis for theme: historic ensemble in place
Land use: commercial, recreational, meeting and amusement center

Project Status

Presently very successful as a result of recent marketing, renovation, and promotion. The decline in use in the 1940s–1960s was not unique to this development, but was a national problem that involved inadequate management and a poor appraisal of the recreation market; it is thus important to stay abreast of leisure trends and the demand market.

SANTA MONICA PIER

The sole remaining pleasure pier on the coast of California (and one of the few in the United States), Santa Monica Pier has survived storms and economic depression. It is the quintessential waterfront development, with users being taken from the water's edge out—literally—over the ocean. The difficulty of maintaining these kinds of piers and the reason for their demise arises from their location directly within storm energy zones. Devastation from the 1983 storms destroyed 60,000 square feet of pier alone in Santa Monica, not including damage to the remaining structure. Many other communities whose piers have been similarly damaged have simply never rebuilt—a national loss.

Santa Monica exemplifies the pressing need for local waterfront development and the need to preserve and upgrade existing facilities. With its shops, rides, amusements, and staging for boat shows and concerts, it remains the hub of the city's tourism industry. Newer technologies are available and are being used in developing oceanside facilities capable of existing in high-wave-energy environments. As the Santa Monica Pier continues to undergo renovation and to improve its recreational attractions, it is hoped that other cities will follow the lead in bringing back their historic waterfront legacies. Pleasure piers make the link to the edge, allowing all people to enjoy direct attachment to the water, regardless of income level—a fact that becomes more important each year.

Project Criteria
Name: Santa Monica Pier
Location: Santa Monica, California
Date completed: major renovations to 1909 original development to be completed within the next five years
Size: 200,000 square feet; 400-foot linear pier
Cost: not available

Description of Project Area Prior to Improvement
Reconstruction of the portion of the pier damaged in 1983 began in September 1987. It should take approximately two to three years to complete this work. Once

Left: Looff Pier (the predecessor of today's Newcomb Pier) is shown here next to the Municipal Pier in the late 1920s. Some of Looff Pier's attractions included the Blue Streak roller coaster, the Circle Swing, the Whip, and the Hippodrome Carousel, which has recently been restored.

this is completed, focus will be on the second phase of the pier's development, which will include 150,000 square feet of new and existing development.

Results of Project Completion

Jobs: not available

Tax base: not available

Events: series of special events on the pier, including dance performance series and kite festivals

Tourism increase: currently attracts 2 million visitors per year. Expects an increase with further development.

Characteristics: provides access to the Pacific oceanfront

Unique Attributes of Project

Architecture and site: pier is local landmark; carousel is a national landmark.

Theme: derivative of the pleasure piers of Europe

Basis for Theme: historic development of pleasure piers on the east and west coast.

Land use: commercial, retail, food, amusement, recreational

Project Status

As part of the waterfront resurgence, this pleasure pier is a success; it is hoped that it will serve as an example for other cities to follow.

Top right: Remnants of 60,000 square feet of the Santa Monica Pier litter the beach in the aftermath of the devastating storms of 1983. The city auctioned off lumber washed ashore in an effort to raise money for the Pier's reconstruction.

Bottom right: After surviving the destructive storms of 1983, the Santa Monica Pier remains today as one of Southern California's major landmark attractions.

MUD ISLAND

Mud Island exists as a unique entertainment "island" in the Mississippi River, offshore from Memphis. Accessible from the city by gondola, its function is similar to that of a pleasure pier. After a spectacular opening with 700,000 visitors in the early 1980s, the facility has experienced great difficulty in later years in attracting more than 400,000 visitors. The lack of attendance forced the island to operate at a loss, and like other similar deficit-run public facilities, its media image was also tarnished.

Mud Island has the potential for success; its major shortcomings are a lack of diversity of attractions and of possible multiple use of facilities, lack of direct access and, most basically, a substantial capital project without the endowment dollars needed for promotion of the facility through the typical start-up period (generally five years). The museum experience is enjoyable, especially the working models of the Mississippi river, but many of these things do not promote multiple visits, critical to long-range success.

The Mud Island development, nevertheless, has spurred over $1 billion in development in the adjacent Memphis downtown waterfront area. As Memphis continues to grow and market itself nationally, and with new additions that will allow Mud Island a wider range of uses and promote multiple visits, the island is likely to become a success!

Project Criteria
Name: Mud Island
Location: Memphis, Tennessee, on the Mississippi River
Date completed: 1982

Size: 52 acres, 227,000 square feet
Cost: $63 million

Description of Project Area Prior To

Improvement

Small sandbar in the Mississippi River, subject to periodic flooding. The development area was elevated 35 feet to prevent this.

Results of Project Completion

Jobs: 330 employees.

Tax base: zero tax base.

Events: daily museum programs include films and tours of the galleries and riverwalk. Special events include "theme" programs such as the Easter Eggstravaganza, 4th of July Birthday Blast, and Halloween Weekend. Festivals include the Catfish Cooking Contest, Folkfest, Neighborfest, and the Kid's Karnival. Ongoing programs include weekly sunset parties, a summer day camp, Campouts/Camp-ins, and concerts. Corporate outings and group picnics are heavily promoted.

Tourism increase: 200,000 new tourists out of 500,000 attendance.

Characteristics: access to the waterfront; $1 billion invested in adjacent downtown waterfront.

Unique Attributes of the Project

Architecture and site: industrial riverfront vernacular; contemporary concrete structures rising from filled river sandbar.

Theme: heritage, culture, and education of the Mississippi.

Basis for theme: Mississippi River as conduit to and distribution center for the entire country.

Land use: leisure and recreation facilities, commercial, and retail areas.

Project Status

Mud Island is a "beacon" on the Memphis waterfront, with 500,000 people attending each year. Future expansions should bring it up to the original 700,000 to 800,000 visitors per year necessary to achieve self-sufficiency. As director Jim Ogle puts it, however: "This architectural wonder has become an operational nightmare. As a very expensive investment, one should seek out as much expertise in future management as possible to understand long-term costs." In planning it will be necessary to be open and honest with politicians, media, and the general public in terms of all developmental, construction, and decision-making aspects of the project. The market, both local and tourist, must be thoroughly researched by more than one source, and competing activities and usages in the general area must be considered. It is also advisable not to make any long-term contracts with vendors for services, and certainly no exclusive agreements because they do not have effective renegotiation opportunities. In planning and design, more emphasis should be placed on daily operations and maintenance than on architectural aesthetics.

50-acre, $63-million tribute to Ol' Man River.

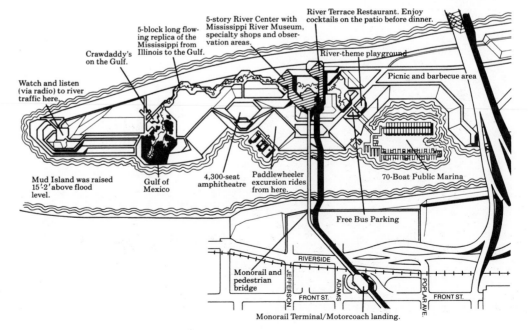

TOWN LAKE COMPREHENSIVE PLAN

The Town Lake Comprehensive Plan proposes a "great park" for Austin, Texas, which would develop over 1,300 acres of waterfront parkland, varying in character from nature preserves to a new downtown waterfront promenade. The intended landscaped quality, in the tradition of the famous Olmsted parks of great American cities, will generate a variety of "events" to be experienced by foot, bicycle, or car, or people-mover or water-taxi systems. A large area will include sites for a number of cultural facilities (museums, galleries, performance halls) within a lushly landscaped park setting. The Pecan Gardens, a family-oriented activity center patterned after Copenhagen's highly successful Tivoli Gardens, combining art, theater, entertainment, and dining facilities within a festive garden setting, is also part of the proposal.

The comprehensive plan makes land-use and urban-design recommendations for adjacent properties throughout the study area, addressing such issues as affordable housing, ethnic neighborhood identity, scenic corridor protection, and public art. In addition, a manual detailing the landscape and architectural features of Town Lake Park lists the following components:

1. *Preserves.* Highly scenic, natural areas meriting preservation or restoration of native conditions.

Top and *bottom left:* As the centerpiece to the city of Austin, Town Lake offers a sylvan park element without continuous access or thematic development.

2. *Neighborhood park.* Intimate in scale, these park areas would house neighborhood amenities, with an emphasis on individuals and small groups rather than on massive gatherings.

3. *The city park.* The great outdoor "living room" of the city, with traditional park activities geared toward the entire Austin community.

4. *Cultural parks.* Places to experience art, theater, music, and dining within a more formal park setting.

5. *The urban waterfront.* The point at which high-density urban development meets greenery and lake with wide promenades and overlooks, affording opportunities for both organized and casual activities.

JOHNSON, JOHNSON & ROY (JJR), JIM RICHARDS, DIRECTOR

JOHNSON, JOHNSON & ROY (JJR), JIM RICHARDS, DIRECTOR

The plan was reinforced by the diversity of needs, aspirations, and visions of Austin residents, expressed through an exhaustive public participation process, which included many formal planning sector meetings; hundreds of interviews and follow-up sessions with individuals and organizations; three city-wide public forums; and the establishment of the Town Lake Waterfront Center, a manned office established for the duration of the project whereby the ongoing status of the effort could be monitored by questionnaires and in-progress maps.

Project Criteria
Name: Town Lake Comprehensive Plan
Location: Austin, Texas
Date completed: 1987
Size: 2,000 acres; 7.5 linear miles of riverfront
Cost: not available

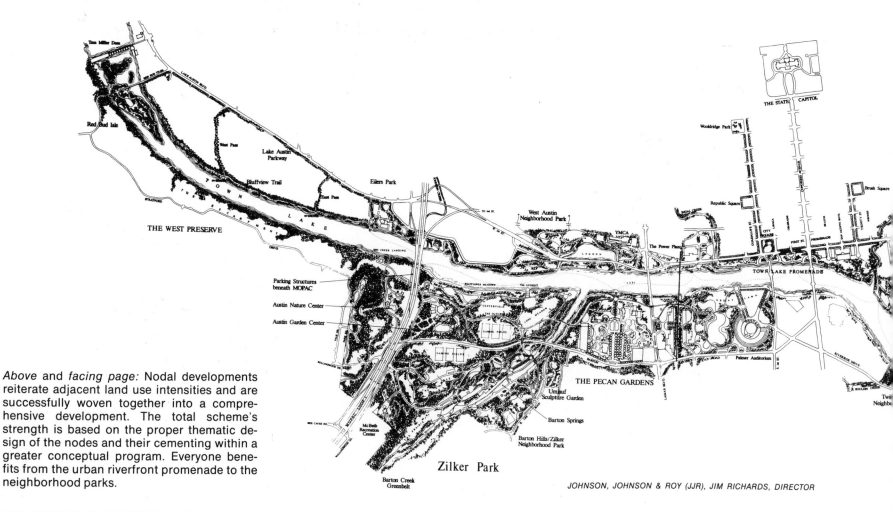

Above and *facing page:* Nodal developments reiterate adjacent land use intensities and are successfully woven together into a comprehensive development. The total scheme's strength is based on the proper thematic design of the nodes and their cementing within a greater conceptual program. Everyone benefits from the urban riverfront promenade to the neighborhood parks.

JOHNSON, JOHNSON & ROY (JJR), JIM RICHARDS, DIRECTOR

Unique Attributes of the Project

Architecture and site: Utilizes what is unique to Austin,—southern Texas neo-romanesque vernacular

Theme: Central park to city of Austin; water orientation

Basis for theme: Five separate park areas that respond to projected land uses

Land use: commercial, office, retail, recreational

Project status

In progress.

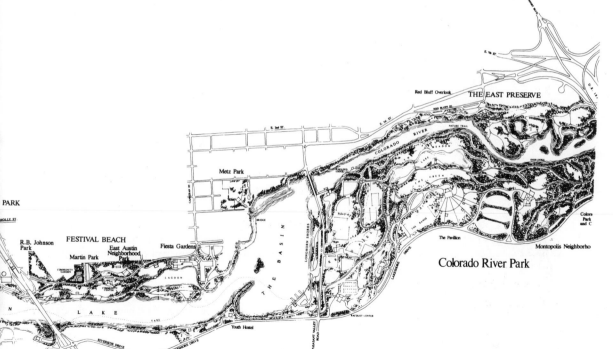

MISSOULA RIVERFRONT

Missoula, a small town in Montana, enjoys the resources of a brisk river running through its core and along its edge. Here, history had allowed some passive recreation to develop, although basically unprogrammed. A competition was held to develop a comprehensive waterfront, one that would create new waterfront activities and also include the elements with which the waterfront development might be able to finance itself.

The proposed plan attempted to correct the commercial core area's lack of orientation toward the river by placing a major promenade at what previously had been the rear of the buildings, creating a second storefront, and then double-loading the area with additional facilities that would step down in terraces to the river's edge. The elevation changes allowed for the creation of a three-story parking garage below, which would provide needed access and parking to both the marketplace, the promenade, and the park area. The stepping down also created an amphitheater, which used the river and great lawn as a backdrop.

The centerpiece of the entire development was the Wintergarden. Like many similar projects, the attempt was to winterize the overall development, making it comfortable and attractive to use twelve months a year. Other important components of the plan were the Baths, a recreational complex featuring hot-spring baths and a sauna, (a regional demand); a riverfront community (leaseback development on public lands, which pay for most of the development costs); and a 20,000-seat arena, serving a regional population and making Missoula a magnet recreation city.

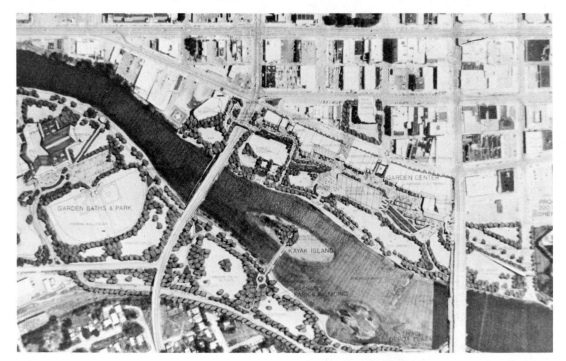

Top left: Turning land use away from direct main street access to a riverfront orientation was accomplished by a parking garage whose upper deck was the riverfront promenade. With Farmers Market *(bottom left)* to thematic Winter Garden *(facing page, top* and *bottom right)* the overall development would be the central attraction in all of Missoula's year-round events.

Project Criteria

Name: Missoula Riverfront
Location: Missoula, Montana
Date completed: competition in 1980, date of projected construction unknown
Size: 1 mile in length
Cost: $50 million

Description of Project Area Prior to Improvement

Underutilized riverfront with downtown retail development's service area backing up to existing park. Lack of parking space and proper access to river.

Results of Project Completion

Jobs: not available
Tax base: not available
Events: festivals, kayak races, holiday celebrations, concerns, theater, and sports
Tourism increase: substantial potential
Characteristics: return of a city to its riverfront

Unique Attributes of the Project

Architecture and site: contemporary architectural approach; infill to period vernacular of existing city fabric, matching date of adjacent architectural style to community
Theme: mountain city riverfront dedicated to year-round use
Basis for theme: potential to turn around retail trade, create market and promenade, center anchor attention of Wintergarden
Land use: commercial, office, recreational, farmers' market

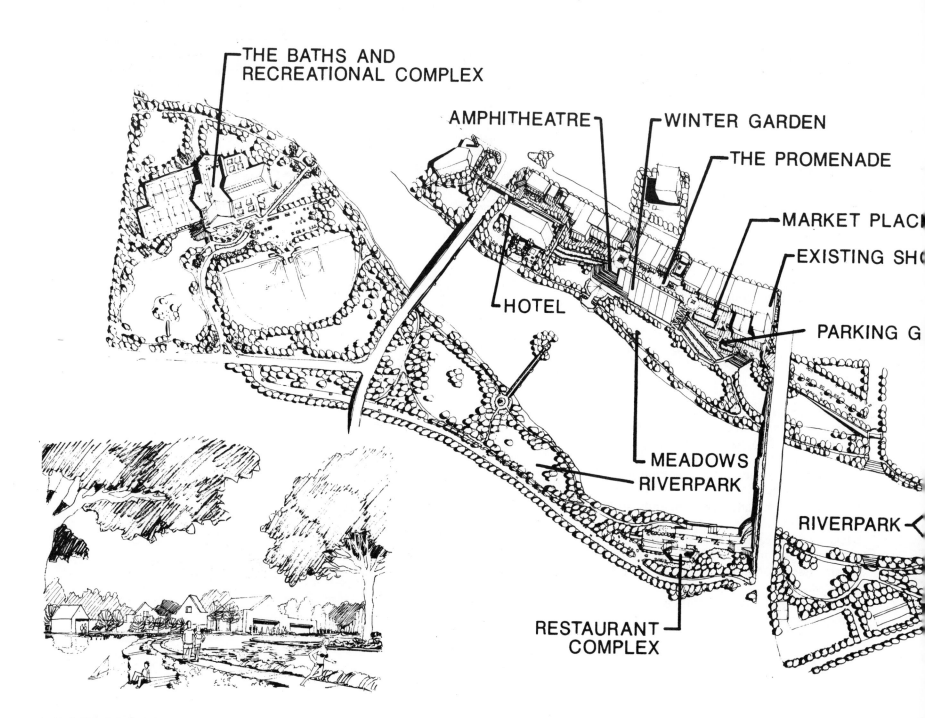

THE BATHS AND
RECREATIONAL COMPLEX

AMPHITHEATRE

WINTER GARDEN

THE PROMENADE

MARKET PLAC

EXISTING SH

HOTEL

PARKING G

MEADOWS
RIVERPARK

RIVERPARK

RESTAURANT
COMPLEX

NEW ARENA

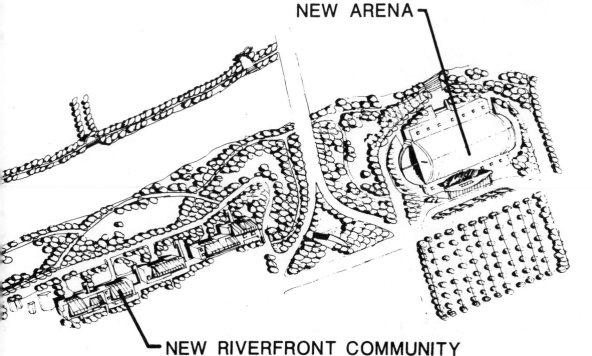

NEW RIVERFRONT COMMUNITY

The composite of nodal developments, (the Baths, Winter Garden, Riverfront Village, and 20,000-seat arena), offered positive economic development with which all components could be realized.

BAYOU SEGNETTE STATE PARK

Located within a metropolitan area of 1.2 million people, this wetland park gives the urbanite direct access to the rivers, swamp, and marshlands, that surround the city of New Orleans. Of its 540 acres, roughly one half (the northern half) is lowland hardwoods, with the southern half a cut over cypress swamp (previously logged), with day use and overnight camping located respectively. A unique feature of the day-use area are the three drainage canals, which meet at the pumping station which keeps the site from flooding. By sculpting these canals into lagoons whose confluence becomes a 20-acre lake, Lac du Segnette, a central image of a water park has been created while the storm-drainage capacity of the pumping complex has been increased by the availability of a reservoir. This central water feature leads the visitor through the site, which includes a wavepool complex, boat launch, cabins, camping spurs, group camp, and numerous trails for fishing, canoeing, waterskiiing, and general relaxation. The overnight cabins were built directly on the bayou and have docks and wooden decks for dining, relaxing, and boat moorage.

As a result of the development, the adjacent land is now in the process of being developed as a full-service marina complex with boathouses, whose operators

Top left: Located within fifteen minutes of downtown New Orleans, Bayou Segnette State Park conveniently and effectively takes the urban dweller to the swamps and marshland that surround the region, providing boat access all the way to the Gulf of Mexico via the boat launch *(bottom left).*

will conduct boat tours south through the swamp and marshlands—all the way to the barrier islands in the Gulf of Mexico. Cultural villages will line the route and provide additional economic revenue along the way.

Project Criteria
Name: Bayou Segnette State Park
Location: New Orleans, Louisiana
Date completed: 1988
Size: 584 acres
Cost: $12 million

Description of Project Area Prior to Improvement
Lowland hardwoods, essentially a cut-over cypress swamp that had been leveed and drained, contiguous to Bayou Segnette, which connects with other bodies of water eventually leading to the Gulf of Mexico (90 miles south).

Results of Project Completion
Jobs: 100
Tax base: zero tax base
Events: holiday events, picnics, camping, hunting and fishing, festivals
Tourism increase: 200,000 visitors
Characteristics: major new nature-oriented recreational facility within the confines of a metropolitan area of 1.2 million people

Top and *bottom right:* The layout of the park successfully creates a waterfront thematic image by sculpturing a lake at the confluence of three drainage canals. The benefits are recreational use and a dramatically increased storm-handling capacity.

Unique Attributes of the Project

Architecture and site: southern Louisiana swamp vernacular; lowland and wetland site development

Theme: Louisiana river community

Basis for theme: historic use of area

Land use: Recreational with minimum commercial; a proposed 13,000 seat arena adjacent

Project Status

The park has opened and exceeded initial projections for attendance. Although its operation could be self-sufficient, it isn't due to the operational characteristics of the State Park System in Louisiana of returning all revenues to the general fund. This is a bad practice which precludes a successful facility in the system from flourishing because it has no control over its resources.

Facing page, top left, bottom left, and *top right:* The architectural theme of the park center and waterfront village is drawn from the fishing industry's historic precedent on Bayou Segnette *(top left)* and has been carried through in adjacent developments *(bottom left).*

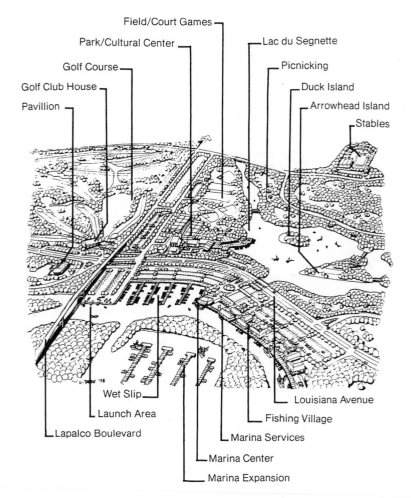

Pavillion
Golf Club House
Golf Course
Park/Cultural Center
Field/Court Games
Lac du Segnette
Picnicking
Duck Island
Arrowhead Island
Stables

Wet Slip
Launch Area
Lapalco Boulevard
Marina Center
Marina Expansion
Marina Services
Fishing Village
Louisiana Avenue

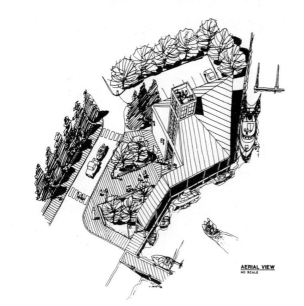

AERIAL VIEW
NO SCALE

Bottom center and *right:* Newer developments proposed by the Jefferson West Cultural Center afford a higher-technology vernacular, separated by the lagoons.

GENE COULON MEMORIAL BEACH PARK

The site's unique qualities combined with the diverse recreational program were the driving forces behind this Washington State beach park site plan. Park facilities relate people to the water and the upland edge. Principal park features include revitalization of an existing salmon stream; eight boat launches with 108 drive-through boat-trailer parking stalls; a marina/day moorage with concession, restrooms, picnicking facilities; and boat-rental buildings, a 900-foot-long "waterwalk" pier extending into Lake Washington with floating picnic shelters. In addition to the waterwalk, there are fishing piers and over 1.5 miles of paved walking and jogging trails.

The architect and owner developed the site use and building program together, assisted by extensive involvement by both the community at large and various special-user groups. One of the primary goals was to create an activity space for informal use by individuals and families that would also accommodate large groups and civic events. By combining the multipurpose picnic and group shelter with the restaurant and boating structure, the developers provided this flexibility, and also created a park that can be used year-round. It was also decided not to turn the new park into a parking lot intended to serve the projected number of visitors. In-

Top left: The architectural vernacular is distinctly northwestern, and the assemblage excellent. Gene Coulon Memorial Beach Park provides a major recreational facility where formerly none existed and asserts its nodal developments amid a complex preserve of passive and active uses *(bottom left* and *facing page, bottom* and *top right).* The architectural theme is both strong in image and logical in function for the overall development. Providing a wide variety of spatial relationships, the park allows the visitor experiences ranging from an active waterfront village to passive boardwalks and trails along the Puget Sound's edge.

stead, overflow parking was designated for accommodation at nearby Boeing plant parking lots. The park buildings were designed to reflect traditional forms of turn-of-the-century waterfront architecture. These are placed in a carefully composed series of formal and informal open spaces linked by both cultivated and wild landscape features such as contoured landforms, open meadows, and groves and avenues of trees. Buildings include a maintenance building and service yard, several large picnic shelters, a restaurant, restrooms, and a boathouse. The multipurpose activity center, containing a plaza, restaurant, and boat shelter, provides a point of transition between the intensely developed southern section of the park and the natural northern end.

Project Criteria

Name: Gene Coulon Memorial Beach Park

Location: Renton, Washington

Date completed: 1982

Size: 57 acres; 1-mile beachfront

Cost: $8.7 million

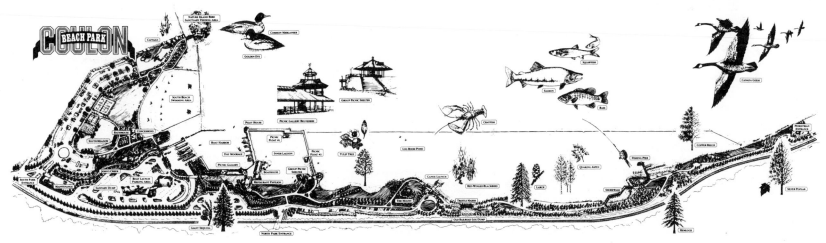

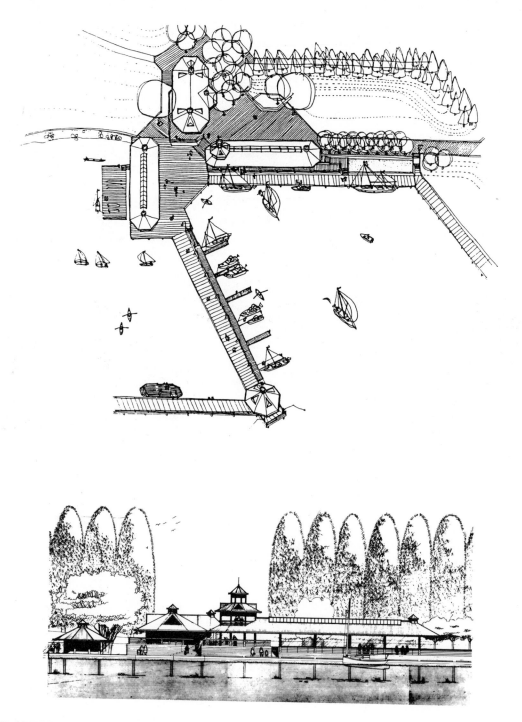

Description of Project Area Prior to Improvement

Historically a horse-drawn coal-barge loading site; later used for log storage, shipping, sawmilling, and ship fitting. In the 1950s it was declared superfluous by the railroad company that owned it.

Results of Project Completion

Jobs: not available

Tax base: zero tax base

Events: festivals, concerts, holiday events, fishing, and recreational events

Characteristics: unused waterfront revitalization offers unprecedented access for a regional population of 1.7 million

Unique Attributes of the Project

Architecture and site: using the Puget Sound as background, turn-of-the-century waterfront vernacular attempts to weave the site structures together.

Theme: waterfront park

Basis for theme: historic relationship of region and waterfront activity

Land use: recreational, minor commercial

Project Status

The park continues to be a major regional draw, stemming from thoughtful, creative planning and design and the use of good-quality materials in the park's construction. One hallmark of the park's success is its low incidence of vandalism. The park director attributes this to the fact that local residents have a strong sense of ownership and pride in the park. The park's major problem, however, is its overwhelming success. On many sunny weekends parking lots are filled beyond capacity, and visitors must spend time trying to find a nearby place to park.

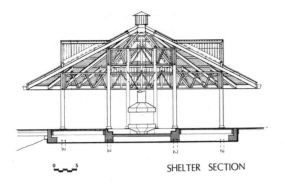

SHELTER SECTION

0 5

Gene Coulon Memorial Beach Park.

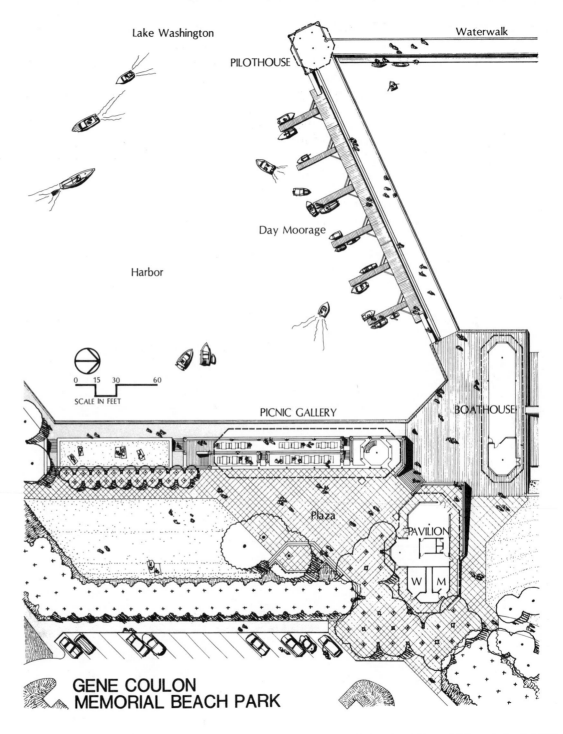

Lake Washington

Waterwalk

PILOTHOUSE

Day Moorage

Harbor

0 15 30 60

SCALE IN FEET

PICNIC GALLERY

BOATHOUSE

Plaza

PAVILION

W | M

GENE COULON
MEMORIAL BEACH PARK

EAGLE ISLAND STATE PARK

Eagle Island State Park is located on the Boise River in northeastern Ada County, on a 500-acre site formerly occupied by the Iowa state prison farm. The first phase, a development of 30 acres, allowed the state to utilize surplus land while meeting the summer recreational needs of area residents. The water orientation helps offset the hot dry summers typical of the region, while the design concept honors the natural and cultural heritage of the land. The development is primarily a summertime, day-use, swimming lake and beach park, with provisions for wildlife habitat and the basic public services necessary to support park use.

The overall design concept acknowledges the historic importance of the area to the Shoshone and Bannock tribes, the current agricultural character of adjoining land uses, and the natural features of a lowland, floodplain landscape. The design is extremely functional, while making a major statement as landscape art. The park has a number of special features. A 16-acre swimming and non-motorized-boating lake imitates the natural oxbow of the nearby Boise River. The bulk of the materials excavated from the lake bed were used to form a high recreational mound at the west end of the site with a topographic effigy mound in the shape of an eagle aş its centerpiece. The eagle, an important symbol to native peoples and a symbol of wildlife conservation in contemporary times, has a 300-foot wing span and can be seen fully only from the air from which it appears to soar eastward. Key eye-level points throughout the site focus and refer the viewer to this large earthwork. Likewise, the agricultural character of the area is reflected in landscape designs that use pole construction, post-and-wire fencing, farm-field layout patterns, irrigation ponds and channels, and native plant material such as willows, poplars, and ashes. Buildings replicate farmstead architecture.

Project Criteria
Name: Eagle Island State Park
Location: Ada County, Idaho
Date completed: 1983
Size: 500 acres
Cost: not available

Description of Project Area Prior to Improvement
Underutilized flat river basin in hot summer plains region, formerly occupied by state prison farm.

Left: The real success of this tiny waterfront can only be truly appreciated when it is viewed in context. An active waterfront and sand beach in Idaho is an oasis, and one which is heavily used. Located in the flat plains, *(facing page* and *overleaf top left),* the effective sculptural treatment of the development deceives the visitor in terms of scale, seeming much larger than it actually is. With its serpentine layout, it is difficult to determine where the body of water begins or ends *(overleaf bottom left).*

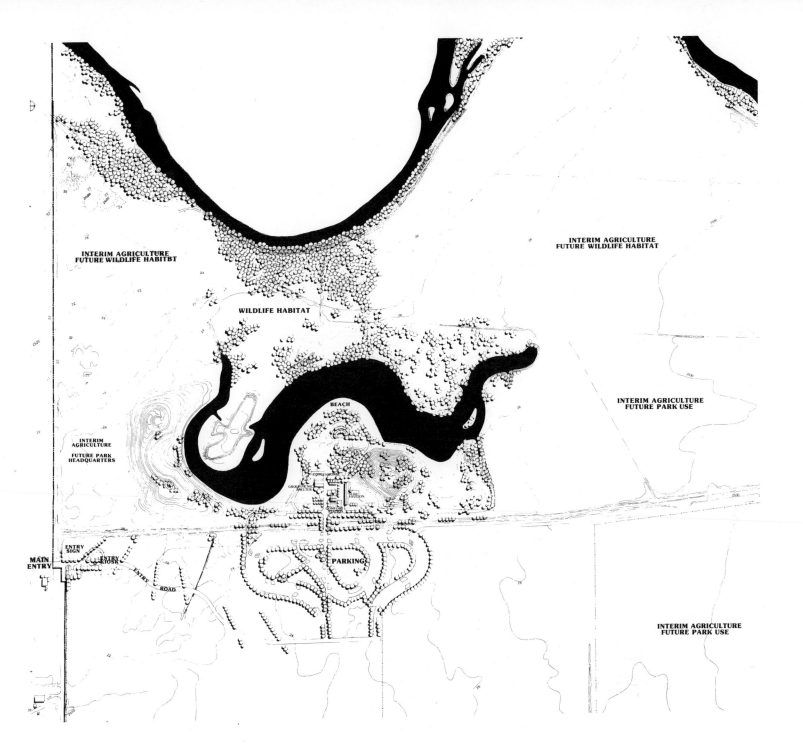

INTERIM AGRICULTURE
FUTURE WILDLIFE HABITBT

INTERIM AGRICULTURE
FUTURE WILDLIFE HABITAT

WILDLIFE HABITAT

INTERIM AGRICULTURE
FUTURE PARK USE

BEACH

INTERIM
AGRICULTURE
FUTURE PARK
HEADQUARTERS

CONE SHELTER

GROUP PICNIC
SHELTER

PICNIC PAVILION

CONTROL
STATION

ENTRY
SIGN

MAIN
ENTRY

ENTRY
KIOSK

PARKING

ENTRY ROAD

INTERIM AGRICULTURE
FUTURE PARK USE

Results of Project Completion

Jobs: 20 to 50

Tax base: self-sufficient operation

Events: swimming, holiday events, festivals, educational and cultural activities

Tourism increase: 1,200 visitors per day in summer

Characteristics: a "waterfront" development in an area devoid of such geographic opportunities

Unique Attributes of the Project

Architecture and site: extensive site work for creation of lake and earth sculpture

Theme: oxbow lake

Basis for theme: adjacent Boise River floodplain

Land use: recreational with minor commercial

Project Status

Figures indicate that the park is heavily used all summer and frequently reaches its capacity of 1,200 visitors per day. Park officials report that many area residents, especially families, prefer the beach and natural environment of Eagle Island to public swimming pools. It is also unusual for a park of this size to be located so near a major city, adding to its appeal.

Acknowledgments

Max Conrad—excerpt from Frederick Law Olmsted Pittsburgh Waterfront Report

New Orleans Historic Collection—Historic New Orleans Photos

Biloxi Historic Photos—Joe Sholtes

Biloxi Working Boats Poster—Bob Landry

Port Louis and Port Grimaud—Chuck Legler

Southbank Riverwalk—Downtown Development Authority, Scott Adams, Deputy Director

World Financial Center and Boston Fan Pier—Cesar Pelli and Associates Fred Clark, partner; Robert S. Charney, senior associate

Seaside, Florida—Seaside Community Development Corporation, Nancy Patrie, Steven Brooke

Harborfront, Seattle—Joann Smith

Pier 39, San Francisco, California—Pier 39, Limited Partnership, Alexis Henderson

Santa Cruz Boardwalk—Santa Cruz Seaside Company, Glenn LaFrank

Santa Monica Pier—Santa Monica Pier Restoration Corporation, Elaine G. Mutchnik

Mud Island—Memphis Parks and Recreation, Jim Ogle, General Manager

Town Lake—Johnson, Johnson, & Roy (JJR), Jim Richards, designer, graphic delineator contact person

Gene Coulon Memorial Beach Park and Eagle Island State Park—Jones & Jones, Susan Huikala

Bayshore Aerial View—Ron Giovanelli/Florida Land Design & Engineering, Photo Credit: Peter Foe

Historic New Orleans Collection

Judy Jacobson—Downtown Development Authority, Jacksonville, FL

Joe Sholtes Collection

Buster Curtis—New Orleans Historic Map

Seaside—Steven Brooke, Portofino—Charles Fryling, Jr.

Tampa Tribune—Bayshore Aerial Photos/ Photo Lab

Bruce Johnson—Bayshore Aerial Photos

Maccaferri Babions—George Ragazzo

Index